And the Beat Goes On

A Survey of Pop Music in America

by the same author

Cool, Hot and Blue:

A History of Jazz for Young People (1968)

charles boeckman

and the beat goes on

a survey of pop music in america

Robert B. Luce, Inc.—Washington—New York

For Patti

Grateful acknowledgement is made to:

The Instrumentalist Co. for permission to reprint a quotation from *The Instrumentalist*, May, 1971.

The MacMillan Company for permission to reprint a quotation from *The Big Bands*, copyright © 1967 by George T. Simon.

William Morrow and Company, Inc. for permission to reprint a quotation from *Blues People*, copyright © 1963 by Leroi Jones.

Nation's Business for permission to reprint a quotation from the article "Country Music Goes to Town," by Rufus Jarman, February, 1953.

Newsweek for permission to reprint quotations from the articles "Mick Jagger and the Future of Rock," January 4, 1971 and "Rebirth of the Blues," May 26, 1969. Copyright Newsweek, Inc.

Contents

1   What Is Popular Music?

In a Nashville recording studio a string band is playing the latest country-western hit. At a high school prom in Dayton, Ohio, teenagers are moving to the beat of a hard rock group. In a housing project in the Watts section of Los Angeles a radio is tuned to a rhythm'n'blues station. In an apartment in Dallas, Texas, a couple puts an album of Glenn Miller records on their stereo, while in an Alabama prison cell, a convict strums a guitar, and in a Greenwich Village pad, a group of long-haired kids groove to a record of folk singer Bob Dylan.

What do these people so widely separated by age, place and life-styles all have in common? They are involved in one way or another with the popular music of their choice, singing, listening to it, dancing to it, and above all, being moved emotionally by it.

It would be difficult to think of any activity more universal and more integrated with the human experience than popular music. Men march off to war to this kind of music. Couples meet, love, part and cry to this music. People hum it as they work. It is music that reflects great social changes and often plays a part in those changes. It can be intensely patriotic, or it can

protest bitterly. It can be a social force as well as a
social and personal experience. It is always the music
of the people . . . the man standing in a depression
breadline, the truck driver on his way to Birmingham,
the Negro searching for an identity in a white society,
the convict on a work farm, the white collar worker
and the blue collar worker.

How can we define this all-pervading phenomenon of human culture, this music that in some decades is bland as a child's lullaby and in other decades
becomes raucous and violent? It is music that can sing
in sweet, lofty terms of idealistic love or it can make
a direct appeal to primitive emotions and instincts. It
can tell about God or suggest to the listener that he
ought to go get stoned on pot.

Sometimes it is played by a big, smooth studio
band composed of highly trained musicians. Sometimes it is played on a five dollar guitar by a wandering country boy who cannot read a note of music. And
the song played by the untrained country boy might
become a bigger hit than the one played by the professional orchestra.

To begin with, here are a few things popular
music is not: It is not symphonic, "serious" music, although some popular music composers have lifted
melodic themes from a classical composition and
made them popular hits. There was a time in the
1940's when Rachmaninoff, Tchaikovsky and Chopin
were very big on the hit parade ("Full Moon and
Empty Arms," Rachmaninoff; "Tonight We Love,"
and "Moon Love," Tchaikovsky; "Till The End of
Time," Chopin).

It is not music sung by church choirs, however

an entire branch of popular music—rhythm 'n' blues —had its roots in the holy roller church music.

It is not, as of today, jazz. Strictly speaking, jazz has become the property of a somewhat select audience of fans who either dig the way-out sounds of progressive jazz or search the record archives for the authentic sounds of traditional New Orleans jazz. There was a time, in the 1920's, when jazz was popular music, and its influence has touched all areas of popular music from country-western to rhythm'n' blues. However, at the present time when young people under thirty speak of jazz they are generally referring to hard rock which is another matter.

If we set out to list the kinds of music that could be described as "popular" we would have to place country-western very high in this group. The effect of country-western—the Nashville sound—upon public musical taste and musical trends over the past twenty years has been profound. It was country-western (or "hillbilly," to use a now somewhat dated term) flavored with Negro rhythm-type blues that started the whole rock'n'roll revolution in popular music back in the 1950's. The hard rock style that resulted from this mixture became the popular music of the young people of the 1960's. A sampling of country-western stars would include Jimmie Rodgers, Hank Williams, Fred Rose, Roy Acuff, Tex Ritter and Ernest Tubb, all in the Country Music Hall of Fame. And of course, the "Grand Ole Opry"—country-western's Carnegie Hall—would have to be mentioned. Country-western music, known by its earlier term, hillbilly, can be broken down into a number of sub-classifications, each with a particular style apparent to a

country-western fan: Western Swing, Mountain, Old
Timey, Rockabilly, Citybilly, Cowboy, Sacred (or Gospel), Cajun, Truck Driver (formerly Railroad), Hobo,
Bluegrass, Ballads (weepers and heart songs can be
placed under this heading), Blues, Breakdowns and
Hoedowns. In a later chapter we examine some of the
differences in these styles.

The ancient art of folk singing revived and made
popular largely by Burl Ives in the 1940's, would also
rank high on our index of today's popular music. Here,
to go back to the elders of the folk singing art in America, we would mention artists like Pete Seeger, Woody
Guthrie, Leadbelly, Josh White, among others; and in
today's protest spirit, Tom Paxton, Phil Ochs, Joan
Baez, not to overlook the poet-singer Bob Dylan, and
of course many more.

Negro blues, once confined to the area of "race
records," are now very popular in music polls. There
were the great Negro women blues singers of the 1920
jazz era, Bessie Smith, "Chippie" Hill, Mamie Smith;
and the country blues singers such as John Hurt who
was recording for the Okeh label back in 1928, Big Joe
Williams, Sleepy John Estes and others. Among the
city blues singers, we have Big Bill Broonzy, John Lee
Hooker, T-Bone Walker and Muddy Waters to name a
few. Music historians trace these blues styles from the
Mississippi Delta country through the prison work
farms and lonesome highways to the crowded city
ghettoes. Broken down into groups, the blues styles
are known by various names such as "classic blues,"
"country blues," and "urban blues."

Of course the hard rock groups who came on
strong in the 1960's and continue to extend their driv-

ing beat into the 1970's, albeit somewhat modified in many areas, are legion, and to list the Beatles, The Rolling Stones, The Grateful Dead, The Led Zepplin, The Jefferson Airplane, would be only scratching the surface. Needless to say, as the 1920's came to be known as the Jazz Age, the 1960's has a good chance to be called "The Age of Hard Rock" by future historians who will see the obvious connection between the cultural revolution of the young people and their music, rock 'n' roll. Rock has its sub-headings too. The "Mersey Sound," the "Motown Sound," the California "Surf Sound," and the Nashville flavored "Rockabilly Sound" are examples.

Rock and folk are especially identified with the young who these days question the old values, the old religious beliefs, the old authorities and ask, is there such a thing as a just war, and is there an absolute morality or is everything relative? But our population does not consist entirely of individuals who are under thirty years of age and feel the need for revolution. There are many others whose scope of memories include the depression, World War II and Korea, and whose bumper stickers read, "America, Love It or Leave It." They are not attuned to the drastic changes in popular music since the mid-1950's. To this large audience, differences in popular music draw the sharp line of the generation gap, and while many of them can appreciate the sounds of rock, folk, and blues, many also think of popular music in terms of the Glenn Miller dance music of the big-band, swing era. It may not be the popular music of the hour, but it is still classified as popular music. And to those who belong to dance clubs, the Latin rhythms of the

samba, rhumba and cha-cha are popular music.
Certainly, show tunes from movies and Broadway musicals as well as ballads by composers like
Bacharach and David who capture the public's fickle
taste for a while must be included in our over-all pano-
rama of popular music. And speaking of "popular," a
recent article in *International Musician,* the official
publication of the American Federation of Musicians,
observes that Lawrence Welk has been called the most
popular musician in the history of the United States.
The writer of the article, Geoffrey Marne, says that
Welk's fans have been labeled, "the Social Security
Set, The Then Crowd, The Whitehairs, The Geriatrics
Generation, and The Welk Nation." But whatever
"square" label is placed on them, they number in the
tens of millions. Welk's national weekly television
show was on for sixteen seasons, the only TV program
built completely around an orchestra to last any time
at all, and in fact a program that was outlasted only
by Ed Sullivan. If that isn't "popular music" we'll have
to redefine our terms.

And then, in the realm of public approval, we
have certain individual performers who seem to set
a pace and style, to hit on a gimmick all their own that
earns them a unique spot in the realm of popular
music. Such a performer is Al Hirt. Hirt, who pos-
sesses incredible technical skill, hails from New Orleans and plays many of the old traditional jazz tunes,
but he is not, to a purist, a Dixieland trumpet man, or
strictly speaking even a jazz performer, which Hirt
himself readily admits. In an interview in the *New
York Times,* Hirt was quoted as saying, "I'm a pop
commercial musician, and I've got a successful for-

mat." And that sums it up beautifully. While many immortal jazzmen barely manage to keep one step ahead of starvation, Al Hirt is cheerfully making millions with a style that the public will buy. Melodies ranging from the old standards of Dixieland to the latest pop compositions are grist for the Hirt mill. He turned to the Nashville sound, recorded "Java" and sold over a million copies, earning his first gold record. It was soon followed by more million-copy hits, "Honey in the Horn," "Cotton Candy," and "Sugar Lips." Hirt is more than a trumpet player; he is a unique personality and entertainer and in part this accounts for his success—but only in part. Largely, he overwhelms the general listener with a facility and flow of notes that cover the musical spectrum the way his three hundred pounds cover the landscape. The public, less interested in a critical jazz analysis than in being entertained, loves it.

Another good example of popular appeal is Louis Armstrong's success in his later years. The average public never heard of his exquisite jazz solos recorded with his Hot Five and Hot Seven. To the man on the street, Satchmo's finest achievement was his recording of "Hello, Dolly!", a pop phenomenon which earned him a place on national polls on top of the Beatles at a time when the Beatles were the biggest thing in pop music, and Satchmo was in his sixties.

Other examples of individual musicians who have captured the commercial, popular approval by their own styles are Liberace, Chet Atkins, Boots Randolph (the Yakety Sax man) and, because of his many commercially successful and highly popular albums, Pete Fountain, although Fountain's clarinet style is also highly regarded in jazz circles. Pete Fountain's place in popular music today is reminiscent of Benny Goodman's role in the music of the 1930's. Goodman could be classified as one of the top commercial successes of his time and also one of the great jazz musicians of his day and of all time.

At this point the question might well be asked, why bother to define or "understand" popular music at all? Why not simply listen to the popular singers on TV, or enjoy dancing to the music one likes and let it go at that. Well, that is fine if one is the type to drift along with the tide, numb from the ears up, without bothering to look below the surface of events to get a peek at the powerful forces that are shaping and changing our world, morals, customs and future. Like nothing else today, popular music is giving us messages loud and clear, and is laying the philosophy of our time on the line. In the most elementary "gut" language, it is telling the listener what today's people think about God, sex, work, race, hair styles, government, drugs, police, poverty, conformity, pollution and war. And, yes, it still tells about the girl next door and what it is like to be young and in love in this sometimes terrifying age of overpopulation, pollution and the hydrogen bomb.

So it might behoove us to take a long, careful look at this complex and sometimes puzzling phenomenon called popular music. When we get through it is quite possible we will have a better understanding not only of the music itself, but also of human nature and the powerful currents that are at work changing our society.

To begin with, some definitions are in order. This

is how Webster defines "popular": "1. Of or pertaining to the common people, or the whole body of the people. . . . 2. Suitable to the public in general; as: a, Easy to understand; plain. b, Adapted to the means of the generality of people; hence, cheap. 3. Having general currency; prevalent . . . 4. Beloved or approved by the people.—Syn. see Common."

That by itself would be a pretty good definition of popular music even if we looked no further. It is music "easy to understand, plain, adapted to the means of the generality of the people, having general currency, and beloved or approved by the people." One does not need a college degree in music nor have to play a musical instrument at all, nor even know a note of music to enjoy and "understand" popular music. In fact, while it helps to be able to sing on key, even that does not stop a bathroom baritone from rendering an excruciating—but to him, satisfying—version of the hit song of the hour while he is in his shower.

So, first, it is music approved by the people in general and having a general currency. Secondly, it is relatively simple. The melody line and chord structure are such that the average untrained ear can recognize the melody and repeat a reasonably accurate facsimile. Joe Doakes cannot leave a symphony concert whistling a Brandenburg Concerto nor can he go around humming the intricacies of a Miles Davis jazz solo. But he can drive home humming the music theme of a movie he has just seen. And he can attend a rock concert and recognize "Hey, Jude." Country-western, soul music, and the majority of the rock compositions use the most basic and simple chord progressions. Some popular composers such as Burt

Bacharach employ chord structures that tend to be more "way-out" by simple standards, yet the melody line remains comparatively simple and above all, recognizable. Try picking out a recognizable melody from a modern, serious dissonant composition such as "Fuvosotos" by Istvan Lang!

There appears to be a need by the general public to identify certain melodies with various branches of music. Thus, to the popular taste, "When the Saints Go Marching In," *is* Dixieland jazz. It is undoubtedly the most requested tune in the repertoire of any traditional New Orleans style band. The musicians might get sick of playing it, but the public never tires of the repetition. This fact is well illustrated by a sign on the wall in Preservation Hall in New Orleans: "Requests, One Dollar. Requests for 'The Saints,' Five Dollars!" In a similar manner, the general public for many years identified the tunes "Perdido" and "How High the Moon" with progressive jazz. Often entertainers have their musical trademarks: Sophie Tucker, "Some of These Days;" Glenn Campbell, "By The Time I Get to Phoenix;" Ted Lewis, "When My Baby Smiles At Me;" Dean Martin, "Everybody Loves Somebody Sometime." Their audience responds instantly to these familiar melody-associations and something in the performance is lacking unless the "theme" is sung or played for at least the one-thousandth time. Repetition is a hallmark of public taste.

The third characteristic we note about popular music is that it is in a constant state of flux, mirroring our everchanging society. One style of popular music may remain in vogue for a while, perhaps a decade or so, and then a new style, along with a new generation, takes the limelight for its brief period. Often, when the new music takes over, there is a tendency to regard the previous style as old-hat or square. The bobby soxers who in panting, hysterical hordes mobbed Frank Sinatra in the 1940's might hardly have believed the day would come when their idol would be regarded as a relic from another age by a generation then in its crib. Yet, to the loyal fans of soul and rock of the 60's and early 70's, those once popular crooners of another day, Crosby-Como-Sinatra, are passé. Their singing is sterile, overly-civilized and tuned to a suspect Establishment, say the revolutionary rock generation who want to hear the rank, bitter, raw emotion of soul tormented by bigotry, hypocrisy and a society the young reject. Yet, difficult as this might be for anyone under thirty to accept today, undoubtedly a future generation will one day look back at rock music as old-fashioned and smile patronizingly at the square old Beatles and those funny Rolling Stones that their grandparents thought were so groovy. (Perhaps even now that coming generation is in its crib, shaking its rattle to a different beat.) The only consistent thing about public taste is its fickleness.

In the early '70's, change is already in the air. Hard rock has been softening. Vocals can be heard and understood. Rock groups are returning to instruments of the jazz and swing days: trumpets, saxophones and trombones. Ballads are high on the hit polls. However, as popular music changes, it carries with it influences of the past, and the rock influence will most likely be felt in popular music for many years to come. And there will be periods of rock revival just as periodically there is a nostalgic revival of 1920 jazz and 1930 big band swing.

The fourth characteristic of popular music is that it is both an outgrowth of its own time and in turn it is a subjective force that helps shape its era. For example, World War I saw this nation in a patriotic frenzy. It was a flag-waving, patriotic atmosphere that gave birth to a collection of rousing war songs. These songs in turn fed the emotional fervor of the hour. Probably many a young man went to the enlistment office bravely singing, "Over There," as his grandfather had marched off to the Civil War to the rousing strains of "Dixie" or "Battle Hymn of the Republic," both popular songs of their respective sides in that earlier conflict.

It is characteristic of popular music, also, that its fans can be placed in categories just as can the music they listen to. The follower of a certain branch of pop music is fiercely loyal to his own chosen sound. He is inclined to look with disfavor and put down either as square or morally dangerous, if not downright subversive, the classification of pop music that does not meet his approval. Hard rock groups think Lawrence Welk should be put in a museum. Welk fans would like to unplug every amplified guitar in the nation. Those who prefer sophisticated big-band swing sound call country-western fans "kickers" and make unkind remarks about the nasal sentimentality of their singers. Country-western fans reply by walking out on a dance that is not playing their kind of music.

We do not intend to participate in such a debate here. Our job is to study the pop music of today, particularly rock, rhythm 'n' blues, soul, folk and country-western; the people who compose and play it; and the underlying social meaning or importance it may have for us.

But first let us examine briefly how the popular music we hear today in the Western world came into existence, how it is composed and performed, and what the currents of social change are that have made it so popular. Then we will be in a better position to understand, "to dig," the artists and what they are saying to us with their music.

Photo—Library of Congress

2 Where Our Music Comes From

Many books about the current pop scene begin with the appearance of Elvis Presley in the mid 1950's. While that event undoubtedly marked a turning point in popular music, the obvious fact is that music has been around quite a bit longer than the 1950's. Probably it has been a part of the human experience since prehistoric times.

The music we know began in Mediterranean countries and later evolved in the European culture. While our popular music has been flavored with American jazz and African "soul," the fact remains that we have imported all the fundamental materials of our music—scales, notation, harmony, chord progression, theory—from Europe. (True, there has been some use of the Indian *ragas* and the sitar in recent pop trends, but this is a specialized area which will be discussed in a later chapter.)

How Homo sapiens first amused himself by making music is of course unknown, but we probably would be close to the truth if we assume that far back in the dim chambers of time, a primitive member of our species pleased himself by humming or grunting in a sing-song manner. So the first instrument was the human voice. Perhaps he also learned to imitate birds by whistling. Rhythmic hand-clapping and foot-stomping accompanied by dancing could be seen in the most primitive cultures and may have followed closely the first singing sounds man produced.

Then our ancestors enlarged upon these natural sounds by the invention of artificial devices, in other words, musical instruments. Again we can rely only on our imagination, but we will assume hand-clapping and foot-stomping were supplemented by hitting sticks together and banging on logs, and thus were born the first percussion instruments which have evolved through the centuries to today's drums, cymbals, marimbas, tambourines, etc.

Next came the wind instruments. Our imaginary cave man might have quite accidentally put a hollow reed to his lips and either sucked or blew and produced a sound much more pleasing than anything he could make with his vocal chords. He promptly found himself in great demand at his tribe's gatherings. From this beginning evolved the whole family of wind instruments. When man discovered how to use metals, it was found that wind instruments fashioned out of metal had a much louder, more exciting, military sound, excellent for spurring soldiers into battle and toning up the pomp and ceremony of parading armies. From these beginnings came today's brass instruments such as trumpets, trombones, tubas, and the reed instruments such as clarinets, saxophones, oboes, etc., all called wind instruments for the simple reason that it takes wind to make them sound.

The last classification of instruments that early man developed was the stringed instrument. Musical historians base this deduction on the reasonable assumption that it took a more advanced brain to coax musical sounds out of plucked strings than to blow on a hollow reed. The piano, harp, ukelele, banjo and the all important instrument of today's pop scene, the guitar, are examples of this final classification. It is an interesting turn of events that until the most recent trends in popular music it was the rhythm and wind instruments that have gotten into trouble with the moralists. Back in classical Greek times, the *aulos,* a wind instrument that probably sounded something like today's oboe, was played for the orgiastic dances of Dionysian rites—the god Dionysus being the god of revelry. Plato banned aulos music from his Utopian state because he thought it would encourage immoral behavior. Trumpets and drums inspired men to get themselves killed in battles. When American jazz appeared on the scene early in this century, it was the beat of the drums and the wailing of clarinets and saxophones and the snarl of trumpets that the keepers of our morals feared were leading the younger generation to perdition. All this time in human development the guitar was the gentle member of the musical family, the property of strolling serenaders, the accompanier of tender love ballads, sister to the harp which angels pluck. But then man learned how to plug this soft spoken creature into two-hundred watt amplifiers and suddenly it thundered out the hard rock rhythms of the sex-drug-anti-establishment-protest revolution.

Returning to the history of our musical forms, we know that as far back as 4,000 B.C., the Egyptians had musical choruses and instruments in the temples to their gods. Music also played a definite role in the life of the early Hebrews. The Old Testament contains

words of Hebrew songs and chants such as the Psalms
and it mentions harps, drums, trumpets and cymbals.

In the Greece of classical times, music was a
highly developed art and science and it played a profound role in the religious, cultural and philosophical
life of the Greeks. The Greeks of that time had the
idea that music could be good or bad morally, that
certain rhythms and sounds were conducive to good
moral behavior while others encouraged, in Plato's
words, "illiberality and insolence or madness or other
evils." Whether this is true or not—and this idea will
be explored more fully in a later chapter—it serves to
illustrate what a powerful emotional impact music
has upon the thought and mood of its own time.

It was, incidentally, in the time of classical
Greece that music was first used in connection with
the theater. The choruses in Greek tragedies chanted
or sang their lines accompanied by instruments, and
we could say this was an ancient foreshadowing of
the opera and stage musical of our time.

The Romans were great borrowers in cultural
matters. Much of their art was copied from the
Greeks, including music, but they developed some
musical instruments of their own, including an early
version of the organ called the *hydraulis,* in which air
pressure for the sounding pipes was supplied by an
ingenious use of water chambers. This instrument
was sometimes played at the arenas of sporting events
—perhaps to entertain the crowd while a fresh supply
of lions was being herded in. Incidentally, while on
the subject of Roman instruments, we might dispell
that old myth about Nero fiddling while Rome burned.
He couldn't have done that for the simple reason that

the fiddle—or violin—had not yet been invented. He might, however, have been strumming on one of the other stringed instruments of that time.

Unfortunately, we have no way of accurately reproducing the music of classical Greece and Rome. Only a few fragments of this early music have been found.

However, while the actual music of those early cultures has been lost, a large part of our musical vocabulary is derived from Greek and Latin. The word "music" itself is from the Greek word *Mousikē* which means the art of the "muse." Other musical terms from Greek and Latin include "rhythm," "melody," "orchestra," "symphony," "chant," "instrument," "scale," and "chorus."

A more direct antecedent of today's popular music than the music of classical Greece and Rome was the liturgical chant of the medieval churches. Later, we'll discuss how church music has played a very direct part in our current musical styles, especially in the areas of jazz, rhythm'n'blues, soul and rock'n' roll. But the early church music of which we are now speaking dates back to the time of Pope Gregory I, known as Gregory the Great, who lived in the sixth century. For some time before Pope Gregory I, the Holy Roman Catholic Church had been using chants, or *plainsong,* in the mass. These chants may have come partly from Greek and Roman music, but more likely from Judaism since the Christian church had its roots in the Jewish synagogues where it had been the custom for many centuries to chant the psalms and prayers. But it was Pope Gregory who standardized these liturgical chants, and for the next thousand years the singing at the Catholic mass was known as the Gregorian Chant.

This church singing which dates so far back in the dark ages has a direct bearing on today's music because it gave birth to an element in music without which our present music would have quite a different sound. That element is the simultaneous combination of tones in an harmonious fashion.

We are so used to hearing our popular music played with the full sound of two, three, and more part harmony that it might come as a shock to some of us to learn that harmony was probably unknown until about 800 A.D. In the music in some parts of the world today, there is no such thing as harmony as we know it. Having no sound recordings of early Egyptian, Greek or Roman music, we cannot be certain they had no harmony or chords in their music. Many historians believe their music was monophonic. That is, the voices sang in unison.

No one knows for sure how harmony was added to the Gregorian Chant of the medieval church, but historians have an interesting and rather plausible theory of how it might have come about. As we know, most of the art and literature of the middle ages was in the hands of the monks. They were about the only segment of the population, including kings, who could read and write and knew anything about music. The monks made up the church choirs. There were bound to be a few monks around who were tone deaf. When they sang the chants they couldn't stay on the melody line, but sang instead a fourth or fifth musical interval below. The sound was not at all unpleasant. It was, in fact, "harmonious," and the choir director decided to keep it. And so the idea of singing in different parts began. Later on, the idea was developed to have these parts move at different times instead of simultaneously, and thus counterpoint or polyphonic music was born. Most of us have sung "Three Blind Mice" in this manner.

Much of classical or "serious" music makes use of this idea of counterpoint. It is also heard in traditional New Orleans jazz, or "Dixieland," and in some modern jazz. This musical device is hardly ever used in the pop music most of us are familiar with, but the idea of harmony is ever-present.

By around the sixteenth century, our present day musical scale of seven notes was in use by composers. Along with the scale evolved "triads," or chords, and the progression of chords. By the end of the Renaissance period, around the seventeenth century, the basic chords had been developed, based on the first, fourth and fifth notes of the scale. In musical terms, these are known as the tonic, sub-dominant, and dominant. It is upon these basic chords and their progression from one to another that most of our country-western, folk, rock and blues melodies are built. This largely explains why it has been possible for young people of high school and junior high age to not only listen to and dance to their music, but to make their own music. Back in the "big band" swing era, when young people were jitterbugging to the music of Benny Goodman and the Dorsey brothers—the pop music of their day—it required considerable musical training and experience to be able to play in a dance orchestra. It was rare to see a teenager playing in such a group and rarer still to see an entire dance orchestra made up of school age musicians. If a high school gave a dance they would hire a band composed of adults. But when the rhythm 'n' blues style of music ushered in the rock music revolution of the mid 1950's, pop music became quite simplified. A teenager could take a few guitar lessons and in a relatively short time—often in a matter of weeks—he could master the simple three chord progression of the blues. Then his pop music truly became the property of young people. They could form their own groups, play for their own school gigs and rock concerts and even compose their own music, and all this added to the cultural chasm between the generations. This may in part account for the tremendous importance and popularity pop music plays in the lives of today's young people. It may not always be great music, but it is their music.

3   Our First Song Hits

It is difficult for us to visualize a time when there were no radios, television sets, phonographs, tape recorders or juke boxes. These electronic music makers of our era shout today's sounds at us from all directions. But in the last century and all the centuries before that, until Edison invented the phonograph in 1877, the only music people heard was "live." Yet there was music a-plenty. Music in the homes, music at band concerts in the parks, music at fiddling square dances, in the slave cabins in the South and the concert halls in the North and the backwoods mountain cabins in the Appalachian hill country and around the campfires of the pioneers who were pushing west. People worked and played and worshipped to the sound of music. And General Santa Anna's regimental bands played the Dagüella—a march signifying "no quarter"—as the final assault was launched on the doomed defenders of the Alamo. Every event in our history had its musical symbols.

Interesting as it might be from a historical standpoint, the popular music field of the 1800's would not be of much value in our examination of today's popular music except for one important thing: certain dramatic changes in the methods and philosophy of mu-

sic publishers took place in the late 1800's—changes
that turned popular music into a gigantic multi-million dollar a year business. This new approach to the
publication, distribution and especially the promotion
of popular music has had a great deal to do with the
kind of music we listen to at the present time. We
shall examine this economic revolution presently.

> "Father and I went down to camp
> A-long with Captain Goodwin
> And there we saw the men and boys
> As thick as hasty puddin'. . . .
> Yankee Doodle keep it up,
> Yankee Doodle Dandy
> Mind the music and the step
> And with the girls be handy."

"Yankee Doodle." The first song on America's hit
parade. Our soldiers marched and fought to that tune
in the Revolutionary War. Who wrote it? Where did it
come from? No one knows for sure. The melody may
well have been around since the middle ages. It has a
bright, rousing lilt and is great to march to. Everyone
loved it. Both sides in the Revolutionary War sang
and played it. Some say a British Army surgeon, Dr.
Richard Schuckburgh, wrote the words during the
French and Indian war in 1755 to poke fun at the
green American troops, but that may be a myth. When
the Redcoats marched out of Boston bound for Lex-
ington and Concord in April, 1775, they kept step to
their military bands playing "Yankee Doodle." But
after the battle of Concord, as the British were beating
a hasty retreat, the victorious American forces, hot on
their heels, were loudly singing "Yankee Doodle." The
British General Gage is said to have exclaimed with

understandable chagrin, "I hope I shall never hear that _____ tune again!"

"Yankee Doodle" became a perennial favorite of all Americans, an unofficial patriotic air. Today, some two hundred years later, it is still as familiar to the average person as our national anthem. However, the tune has found its way into causes not always patriotic, at least as far as the U.S. is concerned. During the Civil War, the South put these words to Yankee Doodle:

> Yankee Doodle had a mind
> To whip the Southern traitors,
> Just because they did not chose to live
> On codfish and potatoes.
> Yankee Doodle, fa, so, la,
> Yankee Doodle Dandy,
> And so to keep his courage up
> He took a drink of brandy.
> Yankee Doodle, all for shame;
> You're always intermeddling.
> Leave guns alone, they're dangerous things;
> You'd better stick to peddling.
> Yankee Doodle, fa, so, la,
> Yankee Doodle dandy,
> When you get to Bully Run,
> You'll throw away your brandy.

As in every period in our history, the popular songs back in the gaslit era of the last century give us an insight into the fads, customs and moral attitudes of the times. It was a period when women's liberation was yet a long way off. Men ran the world, nationalism and patriotism were at high levels, motherhood was sacred, women led sheltered lives and the distinction between a lady and a "fallen woman" was clearly defined. It was a naïve, unsophisticated period, a time of homey virtues and great sentimentality. Listeners were moved to tears over songs about mother, the flag, death of a loved one, little children, a young girl's honor and drunkards who neglected their families for the corner saloon. People could be deeply touched by a nostalgic melody about Ohio or Indiana or life on the old plantation down South though they, themselves, might never have been further south or west than the Hudson river.

Pure insanity in the lyrics of popular songs has always delighted us Americans.

"It rained all day the night I left,
    "The weather it was dry;
"The sun shone so hot I froze to death,
    "Oh, Susannah, don't you cry."

What could be more idiotic than these words of "Oh Susannah," a song loved by Americans for more than a hundred years? It made the "top charts" of the forty-niners bound for the California gold rush. (They changed the line, "I'm goin' to Alabamy with a banjo on my knee" to "I'm goin' to California with a banjo on my knee.")

The lyrics of "Oh, Susannah" have somewhat the kind of delightful goofiness of "It Ain't Gonna Rain No Mo'," which became the first big sheet music and record hillbilly hit song back in the 1920's. In one of the numerous verses of "It Ain't Gonna Rain No Mo'," an old man is described as standing out on a porch in a dark and stormy night with his shoes full of feet.

From "The Three Little Fishies" (boop-boop-dit-tem-dattem-wattem-chu) to Roger Miller's "You Can't

Roller Skate in a Buffalo Herd," we see that same element of utter nonsense. What can this possibly tell us except that one classification of pop songs is just pure fun?

So is dancing. But the style of dancing in the 1800's was infinitely more complicated than popular dancing today. The Minuet, the "Country Dance" (which had nothing to do with kicking one's heels up in the country; it was a misspelling of the French word, "contre-danse"), the Virginia Reel (in England they called it Sir Roger de Coverly), the Quadrille— and finally the waltz which appeared late in the 1800's and scandalized the older generation . . . these dances took a bit of instruction to follow the complicated steps and turns without tripping. So cities and towns of any size all had their dancing masters and music teachers.

Young maidens were not supposed to know much beyond the matters of housekeeping, doing simple sums and being able to read, but the ability to perform on the piano and/or guitar was practically *de rigueur* for a respectably brought up young lady who hoped to win herself a husband. So the music teachers were kept busy, and most homes had a piano or an organ of the variety that required vigorous pumping before it would express itself in wheezing tones. We are speaking of the more populous, settled areas. In the frontier and rural areas there might be a traveling music instructor, but more likely there was not, and so most rural musicians were self-taught, playing whatever they could get their hands on. It might be an accordian or harmonica, or could just as well be a washboard or jug. There seems to be no end to human ingenuity in creating musical instruments out of what is at hand, when the urge to play becomes strong enough.

There were many religious songs, of course, sung in church and at the revival camp meetings. And there were folk songs brought to America from other countries. In the Appalachian highlands, settlers sang ballads that could be traced back to Elizabethan England. Music of the Southwest was flavored with the Spanish-Mexican tradition. Louisiana had its French heritage; and the German, Bohemian and Polish settlements in Texas played the music of their fatherlands. All these strains went into the melting pot of American popular music, and their influences can be traced to the present.

Here's a ditty that, in addition to becoming a rage in 1828, symbolized the beginning of a form of entertainment that swept America with a tidal wave of popular songs, dances, and stories, and later evolved into vaudeville and the variety shows we know today. That purely American invention of the theater was called the minstrel show.

The ditty, "Jump Jim Crow," was made famous by an actor and pioneer minstrel man, Thomas Dartmouth Rice.

"I came from ole Kentucky
Long time ago
Where I first larn to wheel about
An' jump Jim Crow.
Wheel about and turn about
And do jes' so,
Everytime I wheel about,
I jump Jim Crow."

Rice got his inspiration for the song and the dance that went with it by observing an old Negro who worked in a stable in a midwestern town where Rice was on tour with a theatrical company. The colored man had a comical manner of giving a little hop and dance as he moved about doing his chores. Rice decided to put the antics of the stable groom into his act. He blacked his face with burnt cork, wore delapidated clothing and as he sang the song before the footlights, he would wheel, turn and jump in a ludicrous, hopping manner. Soon his song became the fad of the day, and the whole country was singing and jumping about in an imitation of Rice's funny dance. Eventually, the name of the song was given to a series of laws passed in states south of the Mason-Dixon line in the 1880's which segregated Negroes from whites. They were known as Jim Crow laws long after most people forgot the words "Jim Crow" had anything to do with one of our most popular songs.

Rice did more of a single act than a complete minstrel. The first group to usher in the standard form of minstrel shows was the Virginia Minstrels, a quartet led by Daniel Decatur Emmett, in 1843. In addition to being a first class minstrel man, Emmett was a composer. His biggest hit number was "Dixie." Most people think of "Dixie" as the battle song of the Confederacy, forgetting that it started out as a minstrel "walk-around" number.

For about a half century, minstrel shows reigned supreme as America's most popular form of entertainment. They played in every city, town and hamlet. They traveled up and down the Mississippi on showboats, and were imported to Europe with equal success. Their jokes and humor were based on stereo-typed Negro characters usually played by white performers in blackface, although there were also many successful Negro minstrel performers.

A good portion of the minstrel show was musical —instrumental numbers, and songs usually reminis-cent of the romanticised plantation life of the Old South. While minstrels were in vogue, much of Amer-ica's popular music was minstrel music; and one of the most successful writers of minstrel songs was Stephen F. Foster, believed by many to have been one of our greatest composers. If his song writing career had taken place today he might have become a mil-lionaire, but the popular music business of Foster's time was another matter. Some of his immortal songs he gave away and others he sold outright for ten or fifteen dollars. He did, eventually, for a few years, earn a fair income, but there were also times when he could not support his family, and he died with thirty-eight cents in his pocket—all the money he had in the world at the end.

Stephen Foster was born on a day appropriate enough for a man who was destined to write some of America's most immortal songs, July 4, 1826.

He came from a distinguished and well-to-do family in Pennsylvania. Although his best known songs were about the plantation days of the old South and about Negro slaves, he never lived or traveled in the South or had any firsthand knowledge of slave life. His early exposure to the customs and life of the black community were through two Negro servants of the family who sometimes took young Stephen with them to their church services.

The thing that prompted Foster to write plantation type songs was the popularity in those days of the minstrel shows. Foster's biggest hits, "Old Folks at Home," "My Old Kentucky Home," "Massa's in de Cold Ground," and "Old Black Joe," were written on the themes of the slave's love for his master, or vice versa, or a nostalgic longing for the old childhood home. (The songs neglected to mention the dirt floor, the cold wind that blew through the chinks in the walls, or the rats in the attic!)

Foster's melodies were ideally suited for the minstrel's traditional instruments, the banjo, harmonica, tambourine and bones. "Oh Susannah!" is one of the best banjo numbers ever written.

If Stephen Foster had lived and written songs in our time, they certainly would have been of an entirely different nature. Probably they would have been about pollution or the Viet Nam War or women's liberation, and the melodies might reflect a Nashville or rock influence. The point is, popular songs give us an insight into their own times and Foster's songs give us an understanding of the minstrel days and the romantic sentimentality of the gaslight era.

When Foster began writing songs he gave them away freely to musicians and friends. He gave two of his songs to a friend who had gone into the music publishing business. This gentleman published them and proceeded to make $10,000 from their sale. One was "Oh Susannah."

That demonstrated to young Stephen that money could be made by song writing, an occupation eminently more suited to his temperament than the job of bookkeeping which he had at the time. He resigned his job, returned to his family home in Pennsylvania and set himself up as a full-time song writer in an attic studio. He soon became well known in minstrel circles, and most of his songs were introduced to the public through minstrel singers.

He never did make very close personal contact with the South he wrote about so freely in his songs. When he needed the name of a southern river for his most famous song, "Old Folks at Home," he and his brother Morrison glanced over an atlas of the southern states and chose at random a little stream in Florida, the Sewanee. "Perfect!" Stephen exclaimed and put it in the song. Thus was immortalized and made world famous a river the composer had never seen and didn't even spell correctly. "Way down upon de Swanee River" is perhaps one of the most widely known opening lines of any song written in the nineteenth century.

Stephen married Jane MacDowell, the daughter of a Pittsburg physician. It was a stormy marriage punctuated by quarrels, separations and passionate reconciliations. It was during one of their separations that Stephen wrote "Jeannie With the Light Brown Hair," which is believed to have been written for his wife.

By the time Stephen Foster took his wife and daughter to New York to live, he had gained a wide reputation and was earning pretty good money for a song writer of those times. But money slipped through his fingers and he started drinking. Finally, his wife and daughter returned to Philadelphia, and Stephen Foster's last days were spent in lonely despair in a bleak room behind a grocery store where, sick and alone, he made a few dollars writing second-rate songs. He died in the charity ward of Bellevue Hospital on January 13, 1864, at the age of thirty-eight. In his purse were a few cents, all the money he had in the world, and a scrap of paper on which were penciled the words, "Dear friends and gentle hearts. . . . ," probably a line for a song he planned to write.

The ups and downs of Stephen Foster's career, his stormy love life, and the apparent element of self-destruction is seen often in the lives of popular song writers and entertainers. Perhaps it is the tragedy in their own experience that enables them to create in a way that moves others. Ray Charles, the blind rhythm 'n' blues singer, has said that to sing with "soul" one must be personally acquainted with sorrow.

Another hit song writer of the 1800's who had great success with minstrel-type popular songs was James A. Bland, a Negro, born in 1854. He has sometimes been called the black Stephen Foster. "Carry Me Back to Old Virginny," "In the Evening by the Moonlight," and "Oh, Dem Golden Slippers" are a few of Bland's best known compositions. Like Foster, he pursued the "plantation-slave" theme popular in those minstrel days.

Bland was born into a family of comfortable means. His parents were free Negroes, and his father, Allen Bland, a graduate of Wilberforce University, was appointed examiner in the U.S. Patent Office in Washington, D.C. He was the first Negro man to hold such a position. James's father had ambitions for his son to become a lawyer and enrolled him in Howard University. But by then the banjo had seduced James into a life-long love affair with music, and the min-

strel life was in his blood. Most of the best known
minstrels were white entertainers who blackened their
face with burnt cork. So universal was the burnt cork
idea in minstrel circles, even the black entertainers
used it. James Bland joined an all-Negro minstrel
troupe and spent the rest of his life as an entertainer
and composer both in this country and in Europe. He
enjoyed a successful career and made money during
his twenty-year stay in Europe, but he couldn't hold
onto a dollar any better than Stephen Foster. He returned to this country around 1900 and, like Foster,
died alone and penniless. For many years his grave
was forgotten. It wasn't until 1946, after a search had
been made for Bland's last resting place, that the
Lions Clubs of Virginia erected a granite marker at
the site, inscribed with the words, "James A. Bland,
Oct. 22, 1854—May 6, 1911, Negro Composer Who
Wrote, 'Carry Me Back to Old Virginny.' "

Like Stephen Foster, James Bland was a troubadour in a rural, simple age now past. Their songs are
now part of our folk heritage. Probably every school
child in America has sung "Old Folks at Home," "Oh,
Dem Golden Slippers," and other melodies by these
two early hit song writers.

The minstrel days of Foster and Bland bring us
up to the 1880's when a drastic change in popular
music publishing took place. "Tin Pan Alley" was born
and popular music in America became Big Business.

4   Tin Pan Alley

In the early days of music publishing in America, prior to the Tin Pan Alley epoch that began in the 1800's and continued roughly to the 1930's, popular music was printed more or less as a side line by a few conservative music publishing houses who, for the main part, printed instruction and exercise books and serious music for bands and orchestras. Occasionally they published a song of the popular variety that caught on and sold 50,000 copies, but they were not specifically in the business of looking for and promoting popular music.

One of these staid old establishments, Firth, Pond and Company, which began in 1831 in New York City, published Stephen Foster's songs. There were other such music publishers sprinkled around the country, mostly in the larger cities. In addition, some regular printing shops would run off songs through their printing presses between orders for wedding announcements and stationery.

From time to time a popular song printed by one of these concerns would surprise the publisher. "The Battle Hymn of the Republic," "Tenting On the Old Camp Ground," "Dixie," "I'll Take You Home Again, Kathleen," were a few that enjoyed national popularity. However none of these publishers considered

themselves primarily hucksters of popular songs, nor
apparently, did it occur to any of them to go out looking for hit tunes and exploit them in a vigorous manner. In short, popular song writing was pretty much a
hit or miss proposition and nobody was making a
great deal of money in this area.

At this point, we should recall an important fact
about the music publishing field of that day. The
money that was made from a popular song composition came almost entirely from the profits derived out
of the sale of printed sheet music, plus some money to
be made from player-piano rolls. Today, the sale of
phonograph records and the royalties for the performance of a song over radio, television and in public
places paid to the publisher and composer through
ASCAP (American Society of Composers, Authors,
and Publishers) and BMI (Broadcast Music, Inc.) far
exceed the money made by sheet music sales. But in
the 1800's, we are talking about a time when a publisher counted his profits by the number of sheet music sales he made, and the composer by the royalties
based on these sales. Since a song could be printed
for a few cents a copy and sold for many times that
amount, there was a profit to be made, depending on
the number of copies people bought.

So, there was a parallel between the music publishing of those days and book publishing today. Both
depended upon the number of printed copies sold.

It was around 1880 that some enterprising, brash
young men became involved in the music publishing
field and hit upon a revolutionary concept of popular
song publishing. The popular music field has never
been the same since.

These new publishers, instead of sitting in their offices waiting for a Stephen Foster to happen in, opened their doors to the writers of popular tunes. More than that, they went out looking for composers and when they found talent they encouraged it in such practical ways as furnishing free drinks and food, thus making their offices hang-outs for talented song writers.

Some of the reckless young publishers who were going out of their way to nurture popular song writing were Frank Harding, the pioneer in this field who inherited his father's publishing concern located on the Bowery in New York City in 1879; T. B. Harms and Willis Woodward; and within a few more years, M. Witmark and Sons. There were others, of course.

This new breed of song publishers began printing currently popular songs as their chief business rather than as a side line. While they sought out talent and coddled it, often loaning money to song writers in financial difficulties and seeing to it that the composers' thirst did not go unslaked, they were also not above buying all rights to a song for fifteen or twenty dollars and then making a fortune out of its publication. This was not always the case. In all fairness it must be said that reasonable royalty contracts were often negotiated, thus assuring the composer some share of the profits derived from his creation.

Many joined this 1880 "gold mine rush" in the popular music field. In some cases they were business men with little background in music. One was a necktie salesman and another sold hooks, eyes and whalebones. Together, with an initial investment of one hundred dollars, they formed a company that became one of the leading music publishers of Tin Pan Alley. They were Joseph W. Stern and Edward B. Marks. They were the first to put salesmen on the road to call on stores that handled sheet music and the first to print orchestrations of their songs as well as piano sheet music. Many of the early hits they published have long been forgotten, but their song "Sweet Rosie O'Grady" is still sung today. One of their gay nineties sentimental ballads was "My Mother Was A Lady (You wouldn't dare insult me if my brother Jack were here)."

One of Joseph W. Stern and Company's biggest competitors was Leo Feist, a corset salesman who turned songwriter and opened his own publishing house in 1893.

At this point it might be pertinent to explain just what and where "Tin Pan Alley" was. In those days it was an actual place in New York, a short section of Twenty-eighth Street between Fifth Avenue and Broadway. Along this narrow street were crowded the music publishing concerns from which emanated all day the sounds of tinkling pianos. A writer who was preparing an article about American popular music for the *New York Herald* made a trip down to this street one day around the turn of the century. When he heard the rinky-tink "tin-panny" sounds of battered pianos in the publishing houses, he used the phrase "tin-pan alley" in his article. Thus birth was given to a term that, although the tinny pianos of Twenty-eighth Street have long been stilled, has become a word in the English language that everyone associates with popular songs. The term has even found its way into

Webster's dictionary which gives this definition: "Tin Pan Alley: a street or district frequented by musicians, especially theatrical musicians; hence a district devoted to the interests of composers and players of popular music; also the body of such musicians."

Today Tin Pan Alley no longer refers to a specific street in New York, but rather to the world of commercial writers and publishers of popular songs.

In the late 1800's, these pioneer entrepreneurs of the pop music business, in addition to encouraging people to write songs, recognized a basic axiom of popular song promotion that holds as true today as it did when Stephen Foster wrote "Old Black Joe." Simply putting a song into printed form or getting it on a record will not insure its becoming a success. *The song has to be introduced to the public by a performer or a group of performers, the more famous, the better.*

From roughly 1840 to the latter part of the 1800's, America's greatest form of popular entertainment was the minstrel show. They played in lavish theaters in New York, Chicago and St. Louis and traveled up and down the Mississippi on showboats. They went around to small towns in tent shows. They were a uniquely American form of entertainment, an original theatrical expression, and the whole world loved them. While they put on skits revolving around stereotyped Negro characters, a large portion of the shows were "olios" or musicals, and here it was that songs were heard by large audiences, thus making them popular across the nation. The minstrel shows gave employment to many actors and musicians and gave song writers a market for their compositions. It is possible nobody ever would have heard about Stephen F. Foster if the original Christy minstrels had not played and sung his melodies.

At the time the Tin Pan Alley industry got under full steam and began manufacturing song hits on an assembly line basis, the popularity of minstrel shows was fading. However, the format of the minstrel had given birth to a new form of stage musical entertainment, the vaudeville and burlesque houses. Essentially, they carried on the minstrel tradition of slapstick comedy, instrumental numbers and songs. The minstrel was dead, but musical comedy was rising from its ashes. It was largely to these new forms of stage entertainment that the song hucksters of Tin Pan Alley turned to introduce their music to the public.

Music publishers were concentrated in a strategic location in New York City. Almost within a stone's throw of their offices were the gaudy night spots of the "Gay Nineties": the beer halls, penny arcades, burlesque theaters, sporting houses, restaurants, and theaters. Here was located the big-city heart of America's music, everything from Tony Pastor's Music Hall (the leading vaudeville theater in the country at that time) to the Metropolitan Opera House on Thirty-ninth Street.

The music publishers quickly learned that a surefire way to launch a hit tune was to persuade a vaudeville or musical-comedy star to introduce the new song in his act. At first they used friendly persuasion, but this was quickly supplemented with more practical methods in the form of payments and bribes. Gifts of diamond rings, mink coats, outright cash or a share of royalties in the songs were offered. Thus was born the "song plugger," an individual who spent his time making the rounds of the music halls, "selling" or promoting new songs via popular singers. Some of the methods employed verged on the spectacular. If arrangements were made with a singer to "break in" a new song, the plugger might hire a claque to sit in the audience and applaud wildly, demanding encore upon encore. On some occasions, a second professional singer was "planted" in the audience and when the song ended, he would jump up and pretend to spontaneously join in, encouraging others in the audience to do the same.

It has been estimated that by 1905, the Tin Pan Alley publishers were paying a half million dollars a year to have their songs plugged. In the 1950's a congressional investigation probed certain allegations that record companies were paying bribes to disk jockeys to influence their record selections. The practice was given the name "payola." Far from being anything new, payola was invented by Tin Pan Alley before the turn of the century. It was back then that popular music in America became big business, and ever since that time, commercialism has played a very definite part in the tastes and trends of our popular music.

The decades between 1880 and 1910 have been called by such terms as "the ragtime era," "the Gay Nineties," "the horse and buggy days," etc. It was a different world then. There were no hydrogen bombs, no over-population, no struggle over civil rights. Few people other than college professors knew the meaning of the word "ecology." People awoke in the mornings without wondering if the world would still be in

existence by the time they went to bed that night.
There was no sexual revolution. In fact, it was a time
of Victorian prudishness. Men were the undisputed
masters of their homes and their world. Women could
not vote, own property, hold public office, or find
many jobs outside the home that were considered respectable. It was the day of the open saloons, red light
districts, big eaters and big spenders like Diamond
Jim Brady. The barber shops, the saloons, the clubs,
the bawdy houses were the sacrosanct haunts of the
male, strictly off-limits to the female unless she happened to be a "fallen sister" who plied her trade there.
It was a quiet age just beginning to get noisy as men
were discovering how to ride machines instead of
horses, how to fly in the air, send their voices over
wires and make permanent records of voice and music
that could be replayed long after the performer was
gone.

These were days of homey virtues and fundamental religion. Young men were advised to work
hard and be frugal. Young women led sheltered lives
and were sternly warned against the consequences of
temptation.

The songs of that day reflected the uncompli-
cated moral code. Vice was always punished. Virtue
was rewarded. There were no compromises with morality. Loyalty to one's lover and devotion to parents
and country were extolled. Sad, indeed, were the laments over one who sold himself (or herself) for
gold, which seems a bit hypocritical coming from a
music publishing business that was using every trick
it could think of to get its hands on the precious metal.

As a matter of fact, the word "gold" appeared to

hold a peculiar fascination for writers of song titles in those days. There was "Gold Will Buy 'Most Anything But a True Girl's Heart" and the virtuous "Take Back Your Gold." Other songs with gold in their titles were "Up the Golden Stairs," "And Her Golden Hair was Hanging Down Her Back," "Silver Threads Among the Gold," "The Golden Choir," "A Bird in a Gilded Cage," etc.

Popular songs of that age had a sentimentality that seems exaggerated to us now. Themes about death, especially involving mothers or little children, were very big. There were such tear-jerkers, for example, as, "A Flower from Mother's Grave," and "Why Did They Dig Ma's Grave So Deep?" Mom reigned supreme in such ballads as "Don't Ask Me To Give Up My Mother," "Your Mother Wants You Home, Boy," and the final clincher, "Always Take Mother's Advice."

It is difficult now to believe that the public took such sentimentalism seriously, but they did. Audiences wept over laments such as, "A Mother's Plea For Her Son," and tears often trickled down the cheeks of singers as they performed "The Little Lost Child," or "The Pardon Came Too Late."

Complete stories were told in these songs of woe. "Bird in a Gilded Cage" relates the sad tale of a young woman who sold her beauty for an old man's gold. "After the Ball" is a sorrowful tale of lovers separating over a misunderstanding after a dance. "In the Baggage Coach Ahead," which incidentally was composed by Tin Pan Alley's first sucessful Negro composer, Gussie Davis, a story is told about a little girl alone in a pullman coach, crying her heart out. When asked where her mother is, she replies that her mother is in the baggage coach ahead—in a coffin. This song was based on a true incident that Davis encountered while working as a railroad porter. Davis was also the composer of a sob song called "The Fatal Wedding." This tale of unremitting misery is about a wedding that is interrupted when the groom's real wife arrives on the scene with their baby in her arms. The baby dies and the groom, probably much to everyone's satisfaction, commits suicide.

While the sentimental ballad was high in popularity, other types—novelty and humorous songs—also met with a share of success.

There were, of course, many successful song writers of that era and the proportionate number of failures also. To go into detail about all of them would require a book in itself. One, however, stands out from a standpoint of the enormity of his successes, his failures, and his sheer physical bulk. His life reads so much like the melodramatic songs of his day that we must include a paragraph about his life. The man was Paul Dresser, brother of one of America's most famous novelists, Theodore Dreiser, though they used different spellings for their last names. Paul Dresser was a huge man, weighing over three hundred pounds, and every ounce quivered with sentimentality. It was not at all unusual for him to burst into tears while playing one of his compositions. For a while, he was undoubtedly one of the top songsmiths of his time. His hits included, "The Letter that Never Came," "The Outcast Unknown," "The Pardon Came Too Late," and his extremely popular, "On The Banks of the Wabash." At the pinnacle of his success he earned nearly a half million dollars. He married a beautiful burlesque queen, but alas, like the songs of his time, his gold turned to ashes and his love deserted him. By then, broke and apparently unable to write any more successful songs, he ambled around from publishing house to publishing house. He felt certain that he had one more good song hit left in him—and he did. It was finally published, but too late to bring back his fortune. The song was the classic "standard," "My Gal Sal," still known by most people today, but Dresser died a pauper before the enormous sales of the tune could help him.

During this Tin Pan Alley age, almost every music store, department store and five-and-dime store had its sheet music department with a pianist always on duty to demonstrate songs for a prospective customer. Sheet music songs were displayed on racks much as records are today in record departments. A shopper could browse through the selections, choose one or more and hand it to the pianist who would play it. This method of pushing sheet music sales continued until the 1930's.

So important to the success of a popular song was the singing or acting star who introduced it that their picture was usually included on the front cover of the song. For example, in 1900, Shapiro, Bernstein and Company's big hit of the year, "A Bird In A Gilded Cage," had on the cover the photograph of singer Emma Carus. In 1901, "Hello Central Give Me Heaven," published by Charles K. Harris, did not carry a photo of Maud Courney, but it did display her name prominently under the words, "Sung With Great Success by." The next year's hit, "In The Good Old Summer Time," informed the prospective buyer that it was "as sung in A. H. Chamberlyn's Latest Musical Extravaganza, 'The Defender' by Miss Blanche Ring," and carried a photograph of Miss Ring.

In the years that followed, the top hits were, 1903, "You're The Flower of My Heart, Sweet Adeline," (Where would the barbershop quartets be without that one!); 1904, "Meet Me In St. Louis, Louis;" 1905, "In My Merry Oldsmobile;" 1906, "You're A Grand Old Flag;" 1907, "School Days;" 1908, "Shine on Harvest Moon," 1909, "My Wife's Gone To The Country, Hurrah! Hurrah!" The big song of 1910, "Play That Barber Shop Chord," featured the great minstrel singer and comedian, Bert Williams, on the cover.

The songs of the early 1900's were reflecting the passing of an era and the beginning of a new world. There were songs about the new-fangled horseless carriages and the flying machines. Soon, there were the World War I songs, "Over There," "Goodbye Broadway, Hello France," "It's a Long Way to Tipperary."

World War I ended forever the old, quiet age of elegance and good manners. It marked the beginning of a century of social upheaval and violence, an age that has brought mankind some of the greatest blessings and the worst horrors since time began.

Some profound things happened to American popular music during the decade of the 1920's— that ten year binge of prohibition hip flasks, raccoon coats, Stutz Bearcat cars, the Charleston, "flaming youth," and bathtub gin. It was a decade when a type of heartfelt music from the deep rural areas of the South began to spread to other parts of the country.

But, we need to go back a few years. While Tin Pan Alley was grinding out its million dollar hit songs around the turn of the century, a new kind of music was happening down in New Orleans. Born of ragtime, church gospel singing, march music and Negro blues, it was called jazz. Some of the earliest bands that played this music were those of Buddy Bolden, Freddie Keppard and King Oliver. Jelly Roll Morton, an unequalled genius of that early jazz age, was playing his piano in the red light district and writing his immortal jazz compositions. In 1918, the Original Dixieland Jazz Band, composed of white musicians, traveled from New Orleans to Reisenweber's Cafe in New York where they became an international sensation and spread the beat of hot jazz to an eager world. Soon bands like King Oliver's were moving up to Chicago, and Chicago itself gave birth to a group of dedicated young white jazz musicians who played a frenetic style of jazz that was the popular musical voice for a wild ten year period. As the words of a song expressed it, "The Whole World's Gone Jazz Crazy, Lawdy, and So Have I!"

Examples of that Chicago-style jazz age music can still be heard on such albums as Volume 1 of *The Bix Beiderbecke Story, Bix and His Gang*, Columbia, CL 844. A more modern interpretation is *Billy Plays Bix*, The Billy Butterfield Jazz Band on Epic BA 17026.

One could draw many parallels between the decades of the twenties and the sixties. In both eras, youth was rebelling. The morals and values of the older generation were being questioned. The music was loud and driving. There was a general disillusionment of the young with the world they found themselves in. Liquor was illegal in the 1920's, so they drank it in the manner that today's youth "turns on" with drugs illegally.

But while jazz was the music of the hour with the hip generation of the twenties, there was another world of music, too, some of it related to jazz, some not, but all of it far from the artificial climate of Tin Pan Alley. It was music of rural people, some living in isolated parts of the Appalachian hills or on small farms and country towns in Southern states like Mississippi, Alabama and Texas. It was gospel singing and it was mountain music and it was Negro blues, and it spoke eloquently from the heart of a simple people close to the earth and the basic things in life.

Today, from these basic early styles have evolved rhythm'n'blues, soul, rock'n'roll, and country-western, which cover the spectrum of pop music in the sixties and seventies. One can only deduce there is something in the earthy, primitive quality of these music styles that is attuned to this age of violence and uncertainty.

In 1930, a building in New York City was constructed at Broadway and 49th Street. It was called the Brill Building and for a period became the location of Tin Pan Alley as music publishers filled its offices. During the hey-day of the Brill Building, Tommy Dorsey rented the entire top floor. Music publishers such as the Robert Music Corporation operated out of the Brill Building and published hit songs like "If I Knew You Were Comin' I'd 'ave Baked a Cake." The Rachel Music Company published "It Was a Very Good Year;" the Southern Music Company brought out "Lazy Bones" and "Return to Me;" while Mills Music, Inc., published Hoagy Carmichael's "Stardust." Also among the Brill Building publishers were World Music which produced "Daddy" and "It's the Talk of the Town," and Johnny Mark's St. Nicholas Music Inc., which had the big hit, "Rudolph the Red-Nosed Reindeer."

Today, the eleven story building rents offices to accountants, tailors, electronics firms, book publishers, film makers, while the music publishing firms have, for the most part migrated to the East side of Manhattan—Madison and Fifth Avenue. Johnny Warrington, who has arranged music for the Tommy Dorsey band, Lionel Hampton, Les Elgart and Art Mooney, and who still has his office in the Brill Building was quoted recently as saying, "The whole business has changed. The publishers have no power now. It's all in the hands of the recording companies. Now it's a record or nothing."

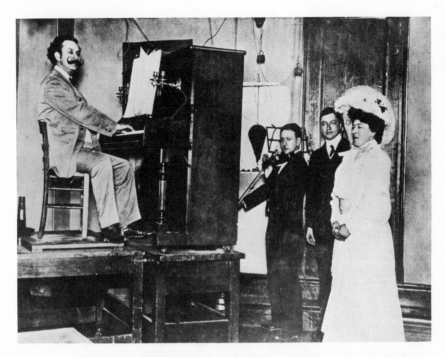

Above, a recording session in the early days of record making. Below, a modern recording session seen from inside the control booth—*photos, courtesy of RCA Records*

5   Singin' the Blues

It gets hot, working the cotton in the Mississippi delta. A man's back aches and the sweat trickles down his body. His hands grow hard as bark from swinging a chopping hoe all day. He's a slave and that is a terrible burden for a man's soul to bear. Then they fight a war and they tell him he's a free man, but he's still a slave to the cotton and the land owner and the company store and never ending poverty, and that kind of futility makes a man's soul cry out too, with its own kind of anguish.

The land isn't much to look at. Mostly it's red clay and when it rains, the back roads are covered with deep, sucking ruts. The levees hold back the rivers, the Yazoo, Tallahatchie, and the Sunflower. Some trees grow along the rivers, sycamore and poplar, and upland, some scraggly pines. But mostly the fields are open and unprotected from the sullen, dusty heat of summer, the kind of weather that saps hope from a man, but makes the cotton bolls swell and burst open. And then the chopping ends and the picking begins.

A man works the cotton fields all day, then goes home at night to an unpainted shack. The yard is littered with rusty cans, weeds, and the rusty carcasses of old cars. Dogs come out and bark. When it rains, the galvanized tin roofs rattle and when it doesn't rain, the tin draws the heat in. If it rains too much, the rivers swell and sometimes the levees crumple and the floods carry whole settlements away. Other times, Gulf hurricanes roar in and smash houses with angry fists and scatter boards around in the water with the bodies of people and animals.

Saturday, a man goes into town. That's the best part of the week. If he's got a couple of dollars in his pocket, he can spend them. Spending just a couple of dollars makes life more bearable. And Saturday nights. Well, that's something else again. Most likely there'll be a dance somewhere and he can get drunk, and that makes life even more bearable.

But you want to watch out. Trouble is always close by. A man feels better carrying a gun or a knife. Never know when a woman is going to make eyes at you and then you're in a fight with her man. Or your own woman catches you messing around with another gal and you wake up with your throat cut. And there's always The Man, the white law, most apt to put you in jail for drinking or fighting or not showing proper respect. That could lead to six months on a work farm and, Lord, a man can do without that.

So, it's a hard life any way you look at it, and violence is a part of it, along with shouting, hallelujah kind of religion, and trouble. Lord, but there's always trouble of one kind or another. Trouble with money, trouble with the law, trouble with the river, trouble with a woman, your own or somebody else's.

That kind of trouble that's always around, well you just naturally cry out about it. You get an old beat-up guitar someplace and figure out your own way to tune and finger it, and you strum it the way you heard some fellow down the road do it, and you sing a story about your troubles. And that's what they call blues singing.

"I need my booze, Lawd, to carry me through the
       day . . . (the long, long day).

"I need my booze, Lawd, to carry me through the
       day.

"Ain't gonna have no booze, Lawd, if the law
       comes take me away . . ."

You don't know exactly why you sing the notes the way you do, but far back in your memory, you can hear your old daddy raise his head and give a field shout, a long cry, with a plaintive break in it, and the work songs that men sang and grunted to in hypnotic rhythm, heaving the dock loads, and even further back, maybe, beyond the stretch of your own mind, to a racial memory handed down in your genes, a dream about how your ancestors sang in Africa to a different kind of music scale from the white man's. All that makes you play the blues the natural way. That's the only way to sing the blues—the natural way.

The minstrel shows of the 1800's, which based so much of their material on plantation life of the Old South and the music of the slaves, were actually not, for the main part, playing Negro music at all. Much of it was written by composers like Stephen Foster who had never been near a Southern plantation field. Of course there was a kind of music the slaves played which was adapted to the minstrels. A slave, having no possessions of his own and very little way of attending functions of entertainment, often devised his own form of musical expression. This consisted first of all of home made instruments: washboards, bones, tambourines and most important, the banjo, an instrument he might well have been familiar with in Africa.

Most slaves, however, were discouraged from performing African music and their tribal dances. For one thing, an effort was made to separate tribe members in order to break up the kind of unity that might result in uprisings and trouble. Also, the kind of heavily rhythmic dancing indigenous to many of the West African tribes could become emotionally exciting, plus the fact that there was a certain element of primitive and sexual abandon in the dances that the owners wished to discourage in order to "civilize" and "Christianize" their slaves.

So, while the African slaves played their own instruments in a style of their own, essentially the music adapted and used in the slave quarters was the European music taught them by their masters. They learned Scottish, English or Irish ballads, jigs, and dances such as the French Quadrille, and the hymns of the Protestant churches. It was this European music given the Afro-American treatment that provided the general style of music heard in minstrels: the ballads, cake-walks, walk-around, spirituals, ragtime, etc.

It is doubtful if the Negro country blues, which is much closer to the Afro-American heritage, was ever heard in the minstrel shows. It is, in fact, a rather recent development. Nobody really put a name to it until W. C. Handy published a song in 1912 called the "Memphis Blues."

It was among the Southern country people, probably in the years following the Civil War, that the kind of folk singing combining the traditions of the field cry, the work song, and the spiritual developed into a style we now call the blues. It was when the slaves became free men and were able to own possessions, among them musical instruments, that many of the musicians and singers began using the guitar, an instrument much more suited to blues singing than the banjo. Having no formal musical education and relying on their ear and imaginative musical intuition, these early blues singers used unorthodox methods of tuning and fingering, which added individuality to their styles. They simply picked up a musical instrument and "fooled around" with it until they could coax from it the harmony that fit their singing. Often it had a primitive, rough quality but that added to the naturalness of their earthy songs. Some of them slid knife blades or bottle necks along the guitar strings to make them wail and sob in a bluesy manner like the cry of an anguished woman.

Many books have been written about the blues. It is a form of music that has been analyzed, dissected, and discussed at great lengths. Music experts have delved into the styles of various country blues singers and made a serious effort to explain every inflection of each note sung. The problem is that blues is an art and not a science, and a very primitive, spontaneous art at that; and one can quickly lose sight of the forest for the trees if he makes too serious an attempt at minute analysis.

However there are certain fundamental elements in the history and style of blues singing that almost everyone agrees upon. To begin with, it is generally agreed that an original form of outcry used by the slaves in the fields could be an ancestor of the blues.

This type of call, sometimes called the field holler, was a high-pitched, wordless cry or chant, and was used as a means of communication between slaves in adjoining fields. It sometimes had a way of rising softly and breaking in a plaintive manner that we hear now in the voices of blues singers. The cry was answered by slaves in a neighboring field and brief messages were exchanged this way. This was later expanded so that more detailed stories were sung back and forth in a call-and-response pattern.

Also familiar to the slaves and probably dating back to Africa were the work songs. Physical labor of certain types lends itself to a kind of monotonous rhythm—chopping cotton, heaving on ropes, cutting wood, dock loading. The simple work songs caught the rhythm of the swinging tools, the straining muscles. It was emotionally and psychologically helpful, and practical, too. Physical exertion becomes easier when a rhythm is established, and the singing helped pass the time and divert the mind while maintaining the work rhythm.

A work song might go something like:
"Gonna pick this cotton row . . .
    "Oh, that row . . .
"Gotta get this pickin done . . .
    "Oh, pick that row . . .
"Gonna pick till the end of the row . . .
    "Oh, yeah that row . . .
"Then gonna start another row . . ."

Again, as in the field chant, the call-and-response pattern is a basic part of the style.

An element common to all blues songs is the mournful, minor-key flavor, the manner in which the singer's voice dips a quarter to a half tone over certain notes, particularly the third and seventh notes of the scale. A widely expressed theory is that the African musical scale consisted of five notes, rather than the seven we have. It is called the pentatonic scale. In adapting his music to the European diatonic scale of seven notes, the African had difficulty adjusting to the third and seventh intervals and tended to flatten these, giving them the "bluesy" minor-key sound, while the accompaniment remains in a major key. This seems like a reasonable theory. And, the folk story-telling aspect of blues singing does seem to be an outgrowth of the earlier field cries and work songs.

In time, the blues developed into a twelve bar pattern using the basic tonic, sub-dominant and dominant chord progressions. The first two lines of the song establish the story the singer is telling about. The last line resolves the matter:

"Gonna find me a woman that stays home every night.
"Gonna find me a woman, Lord, that stays home every night.
"And when I find that woman . . . sure gonna treat her right."

But the blues, like any spontaneous folk singing, is not confined to any rigid musical disciplines. The form remains loose and flexible to adapt to the various blues singers' personal styles, and not all blues singers stick slavishly to the twelve-bar pattern or chord progression outlined above.

As we shall see, this native American form of music, the blues, born in the cotton fields and share-cropper shacks in the rural South, has spread into virtually all forms of popular music, from jazz and swing to hillbilly, folk and rock.

Glen Campbell—*Capitol Records photo*

6   That Old-Time Religion

A large carnival tent has been set up on the fringe of town. It is a low-rent area, a section of filling stations, third-rate rooming houses, used car lots, bars, and delapidated homes. The city hasn't gotten around to repairing the holes in the streets made by heavy trucks. There are some vacant lots in the area and it is in one of these lots that the tent has been spread. Sawdust has been scattered on the ground under the tent and rows of folding chairs arranged, all facing a stage-like platform at one end of the tent. A large banner at the entrance bears the word, "Revival!"

That night, as dusk falls, cars begin to fill the parking area. For the most part they are older model cars and pick-up trucks. The tent is soon filled to capacity. In the audience are people of all ages. Many of the men wear overalls or blue work shirts and trousers. Here and there a seersucker suit is seen. The women wear simple cotton dresses. Some of the teenage girls are in short skirts. It is July and the tent has trapped the heat of the day. The congregation tries to get comfortable by fanning with newspapers and hymn books.

The service opens with a teenage brother and sister team who play amplified guitars and sing. Later, there will be a husband and wife music team who play piano and drums while the congregation sings.

The preaching begins. The sermon is keyed to a high emotional level. There are exhortations, promises and threats, with little coherence to the rambling delivery. The preacher's voice rises and falls, breaking almost into sobs at some points. There is much talk about sin, concentrating especially in the area of sexual delinquencies, liquor-drinking and gambling. Time and again, the congregation is reminded of the frailty of life and the imminence of death. Upon this close of mortal life which can occur at any moment, the congregation is offered two paths. One leads to the pearly gates with rewards of a very earthy nature; the other leads straight to everlasting damnation with various forms of physical torture which are described in detail according to the preacher's imagination and resourcefulness.

As the emotional fervor of the preaching increases, sighs, "Amens!" and exclamations of "Praise the Lord!" are heard from the congregation. An electric tension has begun to charge the atmosphere of the crowded tent.

Presently, the minister will exhort those who have seen the light, who are prepared to renounce their sins and accept Jesus as their Savior, to come to the front of the tent and make public confessions. If the preaching has been successful, a number will do so. They will recite their stories of falling prey to weakness of the flesh. This might include getting drunk, wife-beating, adultery, laziness, various degrees of sexual fooling around, stealing and back-sliding. (A back-slider is one who was saved, but slipped back into his sinful ways.) The stories always include, how-

ever, the fact that the miscreant has seen the wicked-
ness of his ways, has repented and has felt the saving
grace of Jesus Christ.

At another point in the service, an incomprehen-
sible babble of voices will fill the tent as the congregation prays spontaneously in the Unknown Tongue.

Music is essential to the service. When the husband
and wife play the piano and drums, the congregation
sings lustily the rousing, rhythmic gospel songs, often
clapping their hands to the beat. "Oh, Mary, Don't
You Weep," "When the Saints Go Marching In,"
"This Train," "I'm Glad I'm on the Inside," "I'll Go
Marching Into Glory." A jazz band could hardly play
them with a better swinging beat. It seems to be the
more affluent uptown churches with their robed choirs
who drag out their hymns more slowly and with less
rhythm.

Congregational singing plays a major role in the
popularity of the evangelical churches. The rural
church goer may not be able to wrestle with complicated theology, but he can be emotionally and spiritu-
ally moved by song.

When the emotional pitch under the revival tent
has reached its climax, the brothers and sisters, in the
grip of religious ecstasy and exhibitionism, may roll
on the floor, jump about, jerk with epileptic-like seizures, or run shouting down the aisle. Erskine Cald-
well, in his memoirs as a preacher's son who grew up
in the thick of the Southern fundamental religions,
described these orgiastic seizures as "coming through,"
explaining that at this point of "getting religion," the
convert is ridding himself of the devil and accepting
the saving grace of the Lord.

This kind of service still takes place in the South

and Southwest and in the part of the Appalachian Mountains that extends through eastern Kentucky and Tennessee. As the South has become more urbanized in the last few decades, some of the emotionalism has been replaced by a more intellectual, philosophical approach to religion in the larger urban-based churches, but there are still many congregations who follow the old-time evangelist kinds of religion. For the most part they have faith in a personal Creator who is ever present in the lives and affairs of the faithful. Salvation through Christ, faith healing, baptism by total immersion, witnessing and testifying are the important elements of most of these Protestant faiths. With Calvin, they believe that man is basically sinful, but can be saved through grace.

The fundamentalist southern Protestant faiths include Assembly of God, Church of God, Church of God of Prophesy, Church of the Nazarene, the Church of God in Christ, Pentacostal, Full Faith Gospel and the Holiness Church. The Holy Rollers, Snake Handlers and Foot Washers are some of the more primitive of the faiths, while the Baptists and Methodists are the largest Protestant denominations in the South.

The degree of emotionalism and fundamentalism displayed in the churches appears in direct relationship to the economic condition and ruralism of the congregations. The service of a given denomination in a large city church may bear little resemblance to the service of the same denomination in an isolated mountain community. In little unpainted wooden churches and revival tents of the low-rent districts, the economically depressed areas and poor rural sections, emotionalism and uninhibited displays of religious ecstasy are more prevalent, while the big city churches are more sophisticated.

Country-western music has been strongly affected by the religion of this southern area. The repertoire of most of the top country-western singers include gospel songs. Tex Ritter, Jimmie Rodgers, Roy Acuff, Hank Snow, "Tennessee" Ernie Ford, Johnny Cash, and many others—virtually all, in fact—have included gospel songs as part of their programs and records. The preoccupation with death, sin and the troubles of this world that are so ingrained with the life, culture and religion of this area form the basic themes for most country-western songs, and in part account for the melancholy tone of much of this music.

The southern Protestant churches made a great contribution to pop music and jazz in their rhythmic style of hymn singing. Numerous jazz musicians trace their earliest ideas of rhythm to the tempo of gospel singing they heard in the evangelistic churches. Rock-'n'roll had part of its roots in this music. Elvis Presley, who was raised in the Assembly of God faith, was exposed to Negro country blues and Pentecostal gospel singing, and no doubt strongly influenced by them. Glen Campbell is another country-western singer who grew up a Church of Christ member. He said, in an interview written for *Family Weekly* by Gloria Paternostro, "I went to every church when I was a kid, even the Holy Roller church, because I dug the singing."

Negro religion in the segregated South took its own course which, however, parallels the white evangelical church. The major Protestant faith of blacks in the South is the Baptist. Music is an even stronger influence in the black churches dating back to the camp

meetings that swept the South in the 1800's, when the
slaves composed, often extemporaneously, the spirituals that have added such rich flavor to both jazz and
the blues. The strong, hand-clapping, Amen-shouting
rhythm of the Negro church hymns has influenced
southern folk singing in all its forms from blues to
jazz.

Mahalia Jackson, the great Negro gospel singer
who has dedicated her life to glorifying the Lord in
songs, has said this about the importance of rhythm
in church singing: "The true gospel song must retain
the beat originally given it as a manifestation of religious happiness. The first gospels may have been the
source from which the first jazz caught its beat . . .
For me, there is a fundamental joy in everything I
sing, 'cause I sing for the Lord."

Congregational and choir singing taught rural
people another important musical lesson: how to sing
harmony parts. Country musicians for the most part
had little opportunity for formal music instruction.
They had to pick up musical knowledge where they
could, and the churches played a major role in their
musical education.

While we often refer to the Appalachian regions,
in truth most of the entire South was an agricultural
community immobilized by poverty and lack of education for nearly a century following the Civil War. Consequently, the appeal of the fundamental religious
denominations was as great in parts of Alabama,
Georgia, the Carolinas, Mississippi, Texas, Louisiana,
Arkansas and Virginia as in Kentucky and Tennessee.
This area of the South has been called "the Bible Belt."

We are speaking of a people who existed in a low

standard of living culture that fashioned their lives and thinking. These were people who patiently bore the drudgery of hard times from one generation to the next. They were the sharecroppers, farmers and cotton field hands. They cut timber or worked in the coal mines or drove a truck or clerked long hours in a small town store. They were the dust bowl Oakies of the 1930's that John Steinbeck wrote about in *Grapes of Wrath*, and the Mississippi Negro field hands, who migrated from the cruelty of Jim Crow in the South to the despair of the big city ghettos in the North. Illiteracy, pellagra, and tuberculosis constantly stalked their lives. They saw their children die of diphtheria, and their women old and worn out at thirty-five from child bearing and hard work. Schooling for many consisted of a few grades in a crowded country school house where they barely learned to read and do simple arithmetic. For others, there was no school at all. They followed the crops and picked cotton from childhood on.

Their social life centered around the honky-tonks, the country dance halls, and the evangelical churches.

Some of the more isolated Appalachian mountain areas populated by the descendants of Scottish-Irish-English settlers were especially insulated from the mainstream of American culture. Life for these people had changed little since their ancestors came to America. They sang the Anglo-Saxon ballads just as they had been sung in England two hundred years ago and in some areas their language was more Elizabethan than American.

People who always know hard times, who live close to the earth and the bitter realities of life, develop a kind of homespun manner of speech and philosophy. Their religion and faith are expressed in simple terms. They are not so concerned with (or for the main part even aware of) the theories of Freud and Darwin or the philosophy of Kierkegaard as with problems of unrequited love, adultery, death, jail, honor, homesickness, drought, a job in the next county, and a personal God, for these are the things that touch their lives constantly and the problems they must cope with on day-to-day terms. And these are the things they write poetry about and put into their music.

It was with the onset of World War II, in the early 1940's, that a long overdue economic change came to the rural South. Industry began moving into economically depressed areas. Jobs were available in war industries. Urbanization spread. Farmers sought jobs in the mushrooming cities. The migration of Negroes out of the South increased at a great pace. The adjustment from rural to city life, despite its economic advantages, had its psychological problems, too.

Where these people went, they took their music and their religion with them. Both the music and the religion have changed with urbanization, have become more polished, more sophisticated. The country blues became the urban blues. Hillbilly mountain music became country-western and then the Nashville Sound. But the rural, earthy heritage is still there, only a couple of decades away from the old-time religion, mountain music, and the country blues.

Scientific American, Dec. 22, 1877

EDISON'S ORIGINAL PHONOGRAPH

Photo—*courtesy of RCA Records*

7   Country Music Goes to the City

Two mechanical inventions had more to do with the proliferation of hillbilly music and country blues during the 1920's and subsequent decades than any other development in American life. Indeed, these two inventions, the phonograph and the radio, and their various close relatives (television, sound movies, tape recording) have had such far-reaching effects upon the music of our times that one is tempted to wonder what today's popular music would sound like without them.

One man, who was not a musician and was almost deaf besides, has had a greater impact on the direction popular music took in this century than all the Elvis Presleys, Beatles, Johnny Cashes and Frank Sinatras put together. In 1877 this genius, Thomas Alva Edison, wrapped a bit of tin foil around a cylinder, turned it with a crank and recited into a small horn, "Mary Had a Little Lamb." The diaphragm in the horn transformed his voice into vibrations of a needle against the revolving spool. When he retraced the needle over the indentations it had made on the spool of tin foil, the thin sound of his own voice played back through the horn. It was a long way from the complicated high fidelity stereo equipment of today, but it was the world's first phonograph. It cost Edison eighteen dollars to build, and it led eventually to the multi-million dollar recording industry of today. In addition to the phonograph, Edison invented the coin slot phonograph known today as the 'juke box,' and as far back as 1881, Edison had invented the three basic forms of microphones which are used most in broadcasting and recording today. Add to all that the entire motion picture industry which grew out of Edison's invention of motion pictures in 1889, and it is apparent how much this one man had to do with the music we listen to nearly a hundred years later.

In 1895, an Italian inventor, Guglielmo Marconi, tapped out in telegraph code a message which was received a mile away with no connecting wires between the sending and receiving stations. Thus was demonstrated that messages could be sent by electric or radio air waves. And so, these inventions were ready to play their roles in our culture and entertainment fields as the twentieth century began.

Page 485 of the 1897 Sears and Roebuck catalog offered the new phonograph invention for sale under the trademark name, "The Columbia Grand," with this glowing sales pitch:

"The Graphophone or Talking Machine is a most wonderful invention. Thousands of private families are purchasing them for home entertainment. They also afford a most excellent means for money making by traveling from place-to-place and giving public exhibitions."

Edison's phonograph cylinders went on the market at the turn of the century. In existence also were the flat phonograph disks. Emile Berliner had invented them in 1887, and he also worked out the first practical method of duplicating hard plastic records by electroplating and stamping. Berliner merged with Eldridge Johnson to form the Victor Talking Machine Company. Their trademark was the famous white dog who sat before the phonograph horn, head cocked, "listening to his master's voice." The Columbia Record Company was also in business at the turn of the century, as the Sears and Roebuck catalog testifies.

Edison later switched from the cylinder to the disk. He was the first to introduce the long-playing (LP) records as far back as 1927, with platters that had 450 grooves per inch. They were not, however, a commercial success. LP records did not catch on with the public until Columbia brought out their high fidelity microgroove records with 240 grooves to the inch in June of 1948.

In its infancy the phonograph, or talking machine as it was often called, was looked upon as something of a toy. The earliest recordings were more or less of the novelty category. Skits by vaudeville actors, novelty whistlers and some singers were recorded. However, the manufacturers discovered that the public was eager for recorded music and by 1906 the recordings of singers were accompanied by orchestras and by 1910 most well known opera and music hall singers had made records.

Those early recording sessions were primitive when viewed in the light of today's sophisticated eight-track (or more) recording studio equipment. The recording was done mechanically. That is, the singer or band had to play into a horn, thus vibrating a diaphragm and a cutting needle on the master disk, much as Edison had done with his "Mary Had a Little Lamb" recording. Since everyone had to crowd around the horn, the size of the orchestra was limited. Also, there were definite limitations to the reproduction quality and range of sound (the highs and lows) that could be recorded. Those early records have an artificial, tinny sound to us now, much as if we were hearing them over the telephone.

Despite the handicaps, however, the record companies bravely released records of many classical works performed by symphony orchestras, or at least as much of a symphony orchestra as could be crowded around the recording horn. There must have been numerous temper outbursts as performers were jabbed by violin bows and gouged by elbows in such close quarters. But the records were made and sold and in homes people cranked up the spring-driven motors of their phonographs and listened. By 1925 electronic recording had been perfected and the impractical horn was replaced by microphones in recording studios.

Popular songs were recorded too, but mainly by singers from the musical comedy stage and vaudeville circuit. Other than the songs of Stephen Foster, few excursions into the fields of American folk music were made. In 1917, the Victor Recording Company ventured into the jazz field to record the Original Dixieland Jazz Band, probably the first recordings made of jazz music. Collectors say that a few hillbilly recordings were made on Edison cylinders. The first hillbilly string band known to have recorded on the old Edison cylinders was Fiddlin' Bob Haines and His Four Aces. But it was not until the 1920's that record companies began recording in earnest both Negro blues singers and country music. The most important early country music artists to record were the Carter Family and "the father of country music," Jimmie Rodgers.

It was in this same decade of the 1920's that an unexpected doorway to city culture was opened to the homes of rural people. And at the same time, country music began to be heard by city people. In the year 1920, a radio station made its first broadcast to the general public. KDKA in Pittsburgh announced the returns of the Harding-Cox Presidential election and soon after began a regular program of music, news and religious songs (a type of programming many stations still use today). Other radio stations soon joined the pioneering KDKA, and a national stampede to radio was on. The early broadcasting stations were weak and the "crystal set" receivers were weaker. It was not unusual for a radio station to get an excited telephone call from a listener six blocks away, informing the station that they had just been picked up, loud and clear. But soon the simple little crystal sets were replaced by regenerative and then superheterodyne tube receivers, and earphones were outmoded by loudspeakers around which the entire family could gather. Broadcasting stations also increased their power, some eventually to 50,000 and 100,000 watts. The radio bug bit everyone, city dweller and farm laborer alike. Before the decade of the 1920's ended, more than 600 stations were operating, broadcasting networks had been set up from coast-to-coast and every third home had a radio receiver.

The radio had a tremendous effect upon the lives of country people. It ended their pattern of isolation and put them in touch with the mainstream of American culture. As the writer E. B. White said, to rural people, the radio "is a pervading and somewhat god-like presence which has come into their lives and homes."

Almost as soon as radio stations began broadcasting in the South, they programmed "live" entertainment, which in many areas meant square dance fiddling and country singing. One of the first stations in the South was WSB in Atlanta, Georgia, right in the heart of the country and gospel music area. Naturally, local talent made up a good percentage of the programs being broadcast. As other stations obtained broadcasting licenses, they also drew on the hillbilly talent in their area. In no time, the air waves were bombarded with the sound of banjo picking, fiddle sawing, guitar plucking, and mountain singing. The programs were aimed at local areas, but when night fell, radio waves traveled farther and listeners in other states and larger cities heard the broadcasts.

Country music began to draw an increasingly large and responsive audience. Eventually, a new type of program was put together: the barn dance. Whereas the early broadcasts had featured random individual singers or musicians, the barn dance was an integrated program of singers, musicians and comedians. It was a type of country music variety or vaudeville show.

One of the earliest, most successful and longest-lasting of these radio barn dance programs was the National Barn Dance broadcast by WLS in Chicago.

It went on the air in 1924. Appropriately enough, WLS was owned by the store familiar to all rural people, Sears-Roebuck; the call letters WLS stood for "The World's Largest Store." By 1933, the National Barn Dance had become so popular that it was on NBC's coast-to-coast network on an hour-long Saturday night show sponsored by Alka-Seltzer.

The National Barn Dance was followed shortly by what has been called the Carnegie Hall of hillbillies, the Grand Ole Opry. Broadcast by WSM in Nashville, the program has launched innumerable careers in the country-western field and has become the citadel of the blue collar workers' culture in America.

All the raw material of country-western music was on hand when radio and phonograph recording arrived—the fiddling hoe-down, gospel singing, mountain ballads, country blues. This was the traditional old-time music of rural people. But it was the radio broadcasts of the 1920's, followed by the hard times of the 1930's—the Great Depression—that really gave birth to the unified country music that we know today. Probably more than with any other era, country-western became associated with the depression years. During this hard-time period also, as we shall presently see, a branch of country-western moved into intellectual urban centers and eventually became the "protest" folk singing that is an integral part of our musical culture today.

In the CCC camps and the WPA projects, in the cotton fields of Mississippi and East Texas, the textile mill villages of the Carolina Piedmont region, the coal mines in Kentucky, the countless little dirt-road, backwoods hamlets, the unpainted farmhouses without electricity or indoor plumbing, it was country music that filled the empty hours between hard work and going hungry during the depression.

When the dust bowl Oakies left their drought-blasted farms behind and set out for the California promised land with all their belongings tied onto a steaming Model T Ford, country music went with them in songs like "Going Down the Road Feeling Bad," "The Convict and the Rose," and "The Great Speckled Bird."

Some of the old traditional ballads were being replaced by new songs written about the hard times: Bill Cox's "NRA Blues," Slim Smith's "Breadline Blues," and Roy Acuff's "Old Age Pension Check." "All I've Got's Gone" and "All In, Down and Out Blues" lamented depression woes; while "Franklin Roosevelt's Back Again" hoped for better times after the 1936 re-election. Generally, however, the "better times" hoped for in the country-western laments were in a world beyond the grave where there'd be no more six cent cotton to pick, no more dust bowls, and no more depressions.

Songs about hoboes were listened to sympathetically as whole segments of the population hit the road looking for work. Cliff Carlisle's hobo songs included "Hobo's Fate," "Just a Lonely Hobo," and "Ramblin' Jack."

Battery radios in farmhouses and in migrant labor camps were tuned to the Grand Ole Opry and the National Barn Dance and other country music programs. Late at night, the powerful 150,000 watt Mexican border stations such as XERA, XEPN, XEAW, would be heard all over North America, broadcasting

Carter Family and Jimmie Rodgers records between Dr. J. R. Brinkley's commercials about his sex rejuvenation goat-gland operation, Norman Baker's phony cancer cure, patent medicines, Bibles, and frenzied evangelists.

On this side of the border, manufacturers of various products discovered they could evoke profitable loyalty among buyers who listened regularly to country music. One can only guess at the doses of Black Draught, the bottles of Wine of Cardui and the cases of Royal Crown Cola that were sold by country advertising. It was the old medicine show, updated by radio air waves.

If the loaves of bread baked by Light Crust Flour, sold by the country string band, "The Light Crust Doughboys," could be stacked, they might reach beyond the moon. In the same manner, Carr P. Collins packaged Crazy Water Crystals in Mineral Wells, Texas, and advertised their beneficial effect upon various ailments of the gastro-intestinal tract via hillbilly entertainers on radio and in personal appearance tours. He made a fortune for his company while keeping the entire country music fan population entertained.

W. Lee "Pass the Biscuits, Pappy" O'Daniel not only sold flour by the ton with his Light Crust Doughboys country string band, but went on to get himself elected Governor of Texas, mainly through the appeal of his country music band. Programs were aired early in the mornings to reach farmers when they were getting up with the chickens and during the noon hour when they came in from the fields for lunch.

The 1930's marked the beginning of the great migration of America's rural people to urban centers, a migration that picked up tempo during the war years when defense plants offered tempting jobs. This shift from an agricultural economy to industrialization, from country to suburban living, has continued throughout America and especially in the South and Southwest, to the present time and has had a marked impact on our culture and music. A syndicated cartoon by Lichty recently depicted this trend in a humorous manner. Two Russian commissars of agriculture are studying a graph of U.S. farm production. One comments, "Is mystery how America does it! Each year is fewer farmers and each year they produce more corn, wheat, beef and country music!" Truth is spoken in jest. The fact is that agricultural production has, indeed, left the small, independent farmer and has become the big business of large agricultural corporations. A great percentage of the small farmers of yesterday have moved to the cities for better paying blue collar jobs. Hillbillies have become city billies. But when they moved, they took their music with them, and it has evolved into a nationwide pop music expression of contemporary city as well as country life.

The shift to urban life had its emotional impact upon rural people and their songs. They liked the material advantages city life offered, while in song, at least, they remained loyal to the country way of life.

The urbanization process affected very directly not only the style but the instruments of the country musicians. The early mountain settlers probably sang their English ballads with very little or no instrumental accompaniment because they owned few musical instruments. As the frontiers became more settled, they began to acquire such instruments as the dulcimer and zither, and, of course, the frontier's most popular instrument, the fiddle. The reels, jigs, and square dances that frontier people danced to were sawed out on the fiddle. From the Negro slaves, mountain people acquired knowledge of the banjo. The five-string banjo was particularly favored by mountain musicians. The jug and washboard supplied rhythm. Harmonicas and Jew's harps were simple, inexpensive instruments many could afford.

This instrumentation became traditional with mountain music. Purists and traditionalists make this matter of instrumentation a great issue, decrying some of the more modern instruments that Nashville has added. While one can see the reason in preserving traditional styles for their own value, it is difficult to understand why critics get up in arms about changes that come about as a natural process of evolution. One could argue that to get the really "pure" mountain sound, it should be sung with no instruments since that is how it started out.

It was perhaps after the Civil War that the guitar found its way into the hands of country musicians. It may have come by way of Mexico and the Southwest, but probably many country musicians first heard it being used by Nego blues singers. The mandolin was another late-comer, appearing on the country music scene after the turn of the century. Of even more recent times are the string bass and drums, and, more recent still, amplified guitars and bass. It was in the Western swing bands of Texas and Oklahoma and in the honky-tonks that country bands began using drums and string bass to supply dance rhythm. A pur-

ist group of traditional mountain musicians wouldn't
be caught dead with a set of drums in their band.
Drums were banned from the Grand Ole Opry for
some time, and when they were finally permitted, the
drummer was at first hidden behind a curtain!

As country music moved to the city, a whole new
branch developed: the honky-tonk style. Beer joints or
honky-tonks, as they were nicknamed, became popular social haunts for the blue collar worker who liked
hillbilly laments with his beer. The typical honky-tonk
was a rather sleazy looking joint, entirely unpreten-
tious and informal. The interior furnishings would
generally consist of a bar, some tables and chairs and
booths, and a band stand and dance floor area. Here,
in addition to cheap, cold beer and a loud string band,
one could meet members of the opposite sex. Truck
drivers could dance with carhops, mechanics with
waitresses, with little more in the way of a formal introduction than a tap on the arm and a request to
dance. Pick-ups were easy. So were fights.

Honky-tonk musicians learned two important
things: how to play with a strong dance rhythm and
how to dodge flying beer bottles.

The honky-tonk social life naturally engendered
problems of love triangles, beer widows, and sin in
various forms, which led inevitably to a whole genre
of honky-tonk songs such as "Stompin' at the Honky-
Tonk," "I Ain't Goin' Honky-Tonkin' Anymore,"
"Honky-Tonk Blues," "Honky-Tonk Man" and "On a
Honky-Tonk Hardwood Floor."

Honky-tonk music is closely related to western
swing in that both have a strong, persistent beat. To
achieve this, drums, string bass and, eventually, by the

late 1930's, the amplified guitar were used. These instruments caused traditionalists to shudder, but from a practical standpoint they enabled the musicians to be heard above the clatter of bottles, shuffling of dancing feet and loud voices.

Western swing is a branch of country music indigenous to Texas, Louisiana, and Oklahoma dance halls. It developed in the 1930's as a hybrid between country music and jazz. The influences of mountain music, old-time dance steps, popular tunes, Mexican border, and jazz are all present in this music. It was the introduction of the jazz element that mainly set western swing apart from the mountain music of the southeast. This resulted in a stronger rhythmic beat and the use of improvisation or jazz solos, called "take-offs." The "take-off" ability of a western swing musician was often an index to his rating as a performer. Instrumentation in western swing bands differed from their mountain cousins to the east. One might find in a western swing band such untraditional instruments as the clarinet, saxophone, accordian, trumpet or piano, along with the standard fiddle, banjo and guitar. A strong rhythm section consisting of drums, bass guitar and sometimes piano are usually present, all playing a heavy rhythm beat. The dude-western costume is almost universal among the western swing bands.

I can recall a typical Saturday night in a south Texas country dance hall in the 1930's when a popular western swing band was appearing. A crowd of over five hundred people had gathered in a great octagon-shaped wood frame dancehall building in the country. They had driven there in Model A Fords and pickup trucks from as far as fifty miles away. Oilfield workers, farmers, ranchers, small town merchants. In many cases, whole families came. The grandmothers sat on benches around the walls with sleeping youngsters on their laps while the young people and middle-aged couples danced and the old men gathered at the refreshment stands outside, drinking cold beer from bottles and talking about the crops. These people had worked hard all week and when Saturday night came around they expected to put just as much energy into their dancing.

As the evening progressed, the western swing band played everything from honky-tonk laments and unrequited love ballads to "Stardust" (using the wrong chords) and "Basin Street Blues." Since this is a region that clings to the dance traditions of a rural culture growing out of German, Bohemian, Polish and Mexican ancestry, the dance program included schottisches, polkas and waltzes. Also included were typical Texas dances such as "Put Your Little Foot" and "Cotton-Eyed Joe." The "Blue Skirt Waltz" was requested more than once. "El Rancho Grande," with its punctuations of drawn-out falsetto yowls by both the band and dancers, was a high spot in the evening. Another popular Texas dance is the "Paul Jones," in which women join hands to form a circle moving in one direction while men form an outer circle moving in the opposite direction. Upon the sound of a whistle from the band, each man grabs the woman nearest and the circles break up into dancing couples until the whistle blows again. Since this affords one the socially acceptable opportunity to dance at close quarters with any number of unrelated members of the opposite sex, it is easy to see why this dance is so popular.

Musically speaking, the majority of those western swing bands were not very good, though most country-western music historians seem to overlook their musical shortcomings. There were some top-notch bands which played acceptable music, such as Bob Wills and His Texas Playboys and Spade Cooley; however, in general it took a pretty unsophisticated musical ear to put up with the out-of-tune fiddle scraping and the wrong chords which came from these dancehall string bands. Still, musical ineptness did not seem to detract from the popularity of these groups.

It was back then, in the 1930's, that the western image became so ingrained in the idea of country music. So much of today's country music reflects this western flavor, from the "western" style clothes affected by the performers and the lyrics of the songs to the steer horns mounted on the Cadillacs of the more affluent Nashville music stars, that one is almost entitled to assume country music originated in the Old West.

It is true there is a branch of authentic American folk song that can be traced directly to the cowboy of open range and frontier times. Some of these songs were related to the job of riding herd. Cattle at night are a skittish lot, prone to stampede for little or no reason other than their collective nervousness. Cowboys discovered that the sound of a man's voice had a soothing effect on the herds at night. So the cowboys on watch would talk to the herd as they slowly circled it, and sometimes they would sing, making up verses to a tune they'd picked up in their travels. Partly, too, the singing helped pass the monotony of the job, and in this respect their songs were a type of work song.

There might, also, in the bunkhouse at the ranch, be a banjo or harmonica player among the cowhands and at the Saturday night hoe-downs and square dances there were fiddlers. From the herd-riding cowboys, the bunkhouse songs, the cattle drives and lonesome ranges of the Old West there grew a store of traditional songs. Many of these were collected and published by the folklorist, John A. Lomax in 1910 under the title, *Cowboy Songs and Other Frontier Ballads.* Some examples are, "When the Work's All Done This Fall," "The Old Chisholm Trail," "Big Rock Candy Mountain," and "The Dying Cowboy's Lament, or Bury Me Not on The Lone Prairie."

Many folk and country singers have included some of the cowboy ballads in their repertoire. However the type of music played by most contemporary country-western musicians today is a far cry from the traditional cowboy ballads. The persistent western myth associated with modern country music can actually be traced to two fairly recent sources: the western swing bands of Texas and Oklahoma and Hollywood's stereotyped "singing cowboy."

Jimmie Rodgers, often called the father of modern country-western music and probably the most beloved and imitated of all country music singers, helped establish the western image in the minds of country music fans. The last years of Rodgers' short life were spent in Texas. He made many personal appearances in the Southwest and changed his famous railroad brakeman's clothing for boots and a broad-brimmed Stetson hat.

The western swing bands that toured the country dance hall circuits of Louisiana, Texas and Oklahoma in the 1930's added to this growing western development in country music. Since they were playing for audiences of ranching people, they often dressed accordingly. Although the days of the cattle drive trails and open range were long gone, that era was being perpetuated and romanticized by radio, Hollywood and the pulp western magazines that were so popular until television did them in. The western bands capitalized on the romantic appeal of the Old West.

In the final analysis, it was the phenomenon of the Hollywood singing cowboy who really put the "western" in today's country-western music. The first and most successful of these was Gene Autry who became a millionaire by singing western songs between lassoing villains and rescuing ranchers' daughters on the silver screen. No matter how urgent the story situation in a Gene Autry movie—the ranch house might be burning down, the villain might be making off with all the cattle, the rancher's daughter might be facing violent destruction of her virtue—Autry always managed to find time to sing a song or several songs, before the movie ended.

Autry was followed by the equally successful Roy Rogers. Other stars of the musical western include Tex Ritter, Jimmy Wakely and T. Tex Tyler.

The western style trappings worn by these music groups has gradually become more ornate as the years have passed, and less like anything ever worn by authentic cowboys. It has evolved into a distinctive clothing category. Many shops today specialize in western fashions.

The country music of today, especially as recorded and broadcast from Nashville, is a far cry from

the earlier styles described. The Hoosier Hot Shots
spoofed the development in their record, "Them Hillbillies Are Mountain Williams Now!" The music has
become smoother, more palatable to urban ears, and
more musically refined. The musicianship of the performers has improved vastly. Instrumentation has
become varied as the old traditional guidelines were
discarded and skilled arrangers have helped give a
polish to the recordings. As a result, the Nashville
Sound has developed into a leading branch of today's
pop music.

Right, the "legendary" Bix Beiderbecke. Below, clarinettist Benny Goodman, drummer Gene Krupa, vibes man Lionel Hampton and pianist Teddy Wilson, members of the famous Benny Goodman quartet of the thirties—*photos, courtesy of RCA Records*

8   The Era of the Big Bands

To the mainstream culture of America during much of the 1930's and 1940's, pop music meant the "big band sound." It was the swing era, probably America's finest hour in popular music, to borrow a phrase from Sir Winston Churchill. Never before or since has our popular music feasted on such a cornucopia of rich sounds. The quality of musicianship present in the pop music scene reached its apex during that period. It was all too short, lasting from August 21, 1935, when Benny Goodman made his historic appearance in the Palomar Ballroom in Hollywood to the post-war years of the 1940's when most of the big bands broke up. But during that handful of years, unforgettable history was made in the field of pop music.

During the 1920's, groups led by musicians like Bix Beiderbecke, Eddie Condon and Frank Teschemacher in Chicago were playing, as the French say, *le jazz hot*. The New Orleans jazz bands, reflecting the influence of marching bands, had emphasized the first and third beat of the measure, playing their style of jazz with a joyful "two-beat" swing. However, the Chicagoans placed equal emphasis on all four beats in a measure and gave their music a more frenetic drive. Their "four-beat" style came to be known as Chicago jazz. They were essentially small groups, usually five or six men, and they played the music of the Jazz Age. But with the onset of the depression at the close of the 1920 decade, America's restless taste grew weary of hot jazz and turned to the opposite extreme, the saccharine, sentimental melodies of such bands as Guy Lombardo, Jan Garber and Wayne King. For the first half of the 1930's, their waltzes and polite fox trots ruled the airwaves and the dance halls. Jazz was still around, but it wasn't selling.

Big bands were not exclusively a product of the 1930's. There had been successful, large groups in the 1920's, the most notable being Paul Whiteman and his orchestra. Whiteman had a big, symphonic size group, containing at times as many as 34 musicians, and his instrumentation included such exotic instruments as the celesta, flugelhorn, basset horn, heckelphone and euphonium. But Paul Whiteman's band of the 1920's definitely did not "swing." Except for occasional inspired jazz solos by members of the group, it did not by any stretch of the imagination play jazz, although slogan makers were able to stretch their imagination to the point of giving Paul Whiteman the title, "King of Jazz." What he actually played were flamboyant semi-classical arrangements of pop tunes. But Paul Whiteman did an important service for jazz—he gave it respectability. He took it out of the province of shady red light districts and speakeasies and made it a popular music form that need no longer embarrass America. Of Paul Whiteman it was justly said, "He made a lady out of jazz." For this he deserves some kind of title. Besides, he gave employment to some of the outstanding jazz musicians of the day, and was highly regarded by most of them, even if they secretly detested playing his ponderous, stuffy arrangements.

Whiteman is perhaps best remembered for what transpired at a concert he gave at Aeolian Hall in New York City on February 12, 1924. At that concert he premiered a symphonic jazz work he had commissioned a young composer to write. The composition was *Rhapsody in Blue* and the composer was George Gershwin. It was the first time that shady lady called jazz had the temerity to set foot inside a serious concert hall, and it became an historic moment for jazz. Even if a purist might justifiably question the validity of calling *Rhapsody in Blue* real jazz, at least it was responsible for making jazz acceptable in polite parlors of respectable people. Paul Whiteman is also remembered for a certain young singer in his band—one of a group called the Rhythm Boys—whose name was Bing Crosby.

Included in Whiteman's orchestra at one time or another were such outstanding jazz musicians as Bix Beiderbecke, Jimmy and Tommy Dorsey, Jack and Charlie Teagarden, Frankie Trumbauer, Joe Venuti and Eddie Lang. Their brilliant solo work managed here and there to shine through the pompous orchestrations like a breath of fresh air in a heavy smog.

But the Whiteman aggregation as a whole did not swing. Neither did other popular commercial large bands of the 1920's and early 1930's such as Ben Bernie, Isham Jones, Hal Kemp, Ted Weems, Vincent Lopez, Fred Waring.

While the sweet, "schmaltzy" bands were cater-

ing to the pop taste of the hour, a few bands—Bennie
Moton, Duke Ellington, Fletcher Henderson, and Mc-
Kinney's Cotton Pickers—were developing a style of
playing jazz with large band ensembles. Jazz, performed by the early New Orleans and Chicago bands,
had been a matter of collective improvising. This
worked with groups of five or six men. But when the
bands grew to as much as 16 men, individuality had
to give way to teamwork. Improvising and head arrangements (patterns of playing a tune worked out
among the musicians as they played) were supplanted
by written scores. Performers learned to blend their
tones until a section of four or five saxophones
sounded like one jazz soloist. The effect of these large
bands with their full sections of saxophones, trumpets, trombones and rhythm instruments, playing
with concerted rhythmic drive and emotional intensity, was electrifying. Their power was thrilling. The
idea of the jazz solo was incorporated into these big
band arrangements, but now the soloist had the additional inspiration of being backed up by the group
playing a foundation of rhythmic patterns behind
him. In the ensemble choruses the saxophone section
would trade phrases with the brass section in a call
and response pattern that had its tradition deep in
jazz roots as far back as the slave field hollers and
early blues. The "riff" became a popular device of the
big bands. It is a short musical phrase repeated over
and over. Tunes like the "One O'clock Jump," "In the
Mood," "Tuxedo Junction" and "Woodchoppers Ball"
are examples of popular swing numbers that grow out
of repeated riffs. Many of these riff tunes were based

on the old reliable blues chord progression—the tonic, sub-dominant and dominant chords.

A key figure in big band swing was the arranger. Upon his skill depended the personalized sound of the band. He not only had to have a thorough knowledge of harmony and theory, but had to know how to "voice" the instrumentation to produce certain desired sound qualities. Proper voicing could make a big band section sound rich; poor voicing could result in a thin or empty sound. The distinctive Glenn Miller sound was created by the way he voiced the clarinet in its upper register to blend in harmonic relationship with the saxophones.

Top arrangers were sought after and paid high salaries by big band leaders. For example, when Tommy Dorsey got a tip that arranger Sy Oliver was leaving the Jimmy Lunceford band, he offered to better by $5,000 a year whatever Lunceford had been paying Oliver. As a result, Sy Oliver went to work for Dorsey and wrote some of his greatest arrangements.

The early top arrangers include Fletcher Henderson, Duke Ellington and Don Redman. Some others who wrote for the big bands were Paul Weston, Ray Conniff, Henry Mancini, Gordon Jenkins, John Scott Trotter, Eddie Sauter, Bob Haggart, Deane Kincaide, Billy Strayhorn.

While Bennie Moton in Kansas City, Duke Ellington in Harlem, and Glen Gray and the Casa Loma Orchestra among the collegiate set were pioneering the big band swing sound in the early 1930's, it remained the destiny of an absent-minded, bespectacled clarinet player with a shy grin, Benny Goodman, to successfully introduce this next phase of popular music to America. In the process he became the "king of swing," and shaped the culture of an entire generation of kids. He was their hero.

Goodman, to begin with, is a highly skilled, thoroughly trained and schooled virtuoso. He is as competent playing the Mozart Clarinet Concerto with the New York Philharmonic Orchestra as he is fingering a hot clarinet jazz solo at some after-hours jam session. He started playing with jazz bands in Chicago while still in knee-britches (had his first professional job at age twelve), then went to New York in the late 1920's, played with various jazz groups and studio bands, and then in 1935, organized his own big band. Having cut his eye teeth on Chicago jazz, Goodman did not go the accepted route of the dull, "sweet" style that was riding the peak of popularity. He determined to have a band that swung in the style of the ones down in Harlem and he acquired the necessary arrangements from Fletcher Henderson. He made a few records for Columbia and played a weekly radio program sponsored by the National Biscuit Company. But his first dance bookings were outstanding failures. When he appeared at the Grill Room of the Roosevelt Hotel in New York, he was given his two weeks' notice on the opening night by the disgruntled manager. The band then embarked on a cross country tour that was marked by a series of flops. In Denver, Colorado, people who came to the dance wanted their money back and the manager demanded that the band cut out that new-fangled swing garbage and play some waltzes.

It was a demoralized band that crept into the Palomar ballroom in Hollywood on August 21. Thinking the band was on the verge of folding up anyway, Benny pulled out their hottest arrangements in what might have been a gesture of final defiance. Probably the most surprised person in Hollywood that night was Benny Goodman when the young crowd responded with wild clapping, whistling enthusiasm. They crowded around the bandstand, screaming for more. A coast-to-coast broadcast from the Palomar let the rest of the nation know what was happening. Suddenly, Benny Goodman and his swing music became the new pop music rage. That quickly can America's fickle taste in popular music seize on a new sound and become totally obsessed with it.

Goodman's popularity increased and in the spring of 1937, his orchestra played at the Paramount theater in New York to a crowd of 29,000 hysterical young people. They screamed and danced in the aisles and extra police were rushed down to help contain their exuberance. Not until the rock festivals of the 1960's, particularly Woodstock, would a young generation experience such a collective cultural experience.

Many of today's young people, having been told of the hardships of the depression, believe the 1930's to have been a totally grim decade. This is not altogether true. The really bleak years were the dark days of 1930–31–32, when people were starving on park benches or standing in breadlines, and banks were failing all over the country. The poignant song of the hour was "Brother Can You Spare a Dime?" One of its touching verses is sung by a fellow named Al who reminds the listener he was a kid with the drum who went marching to France in 1918 and now he's begging for a dime.

But in 1932, Franklin D. Roosevelt was elected president and his "New Deal" imbued a whole nation with renewed hope. Whatever his critics say, it must be admitted that Roosevelt's cheerful grin and unquenchable confidence made everyone feel better. He was a superb father figure for the entire nation. After listening to one of his famous fireside chats on the radio, one had the feeling that everything was going to be all right—even if you couldn't always put your finger on exactly what it was he'd said. In a practical sense, while prosperity didn't actually return until the war years, the Roosevelt administration had to some extent chased the wolf from the door. There was the WPA and the CCC camps and relief checks to keep people from starving, and the word "repeal" meant prohibition had been done away with.

Too, while Hitler and Mussolini had everyone worried, nuclear warfare had not yet been developed, overpopulation was only a theory of a chap named Malthus and pollution was still far around the corner. If anything, the hardships of the depression had drawn the nation closer, nearly everyone being in the same leaky boat.

So, when the big bands with their lively, infectious swing appeared on the scene, they were welcomed by young people who liked to dance and have a good time. America, though hungry, still knew how to laugh.

If you were young enough and a real hep cat with sufficient energy, the music sent you out of this world and you cut a rug doing the jitterbug, the Big Apple, the Lindy Hop, and you went truckin' on down.

Or you parked with your best girl, turned on the car radio and listened to one of the big bands broadcasting live from magic places like the Aragon Ballroom in Chicago, the Hotel Roosevelt in New Orleans or the Mark Hopkins Hotel in San Francisco.

Just as record sales are the life blood of today's pop music field, live radio broadcasts played a vital role in the saga of the big bands. In addition to going on the air from such dance palaces as Frank Dailey's Meadowbrook, Glen Island Casino, the Hotel Sherman and the Palladium, big bands appeared on sponsored, prime-time network radio shows almost nightly, reaching vast audiences. These shows included the Fitch Bandwagon which presented a parade of top bands and the Camel Caravan on which Benny Goodman appeared. Philip Morris sponsored the Horace Heidt program while Old Gold presented bands like Paul Whiteman, Larry Clinton, Frankie Carl, Artie Shaw and Woody Herman. Kay Kyser's College of Musical Knowledge was highly popular as was the Lucky Strike Hit Parade.

The large bands recorded on the low-fi, cumbersome 78 rpm records of that day (there were only three major recording companies: RCA, Columbia and Decca as compared to dozens today), but recordings were not nearly so important to the success of the pop stars then as now. Radio was the thing. In the summer season of 1939 alone, 70 bands were broadcasting over the NBC and CBS networks, plus still more on Mutual. Radio was much more a consistent friend and enthusiastic booster of pop music than television has ever been.

The musical heroes of the kids of that bygone

day, in addition to Benny Goodman with his brilliant, driving clarinet, were Tommy Dorsey with his high, sweet trombone, Gene Krupa and his frenetic drums, and Harry James blowing his flashy trumpet style. Popularity of the swing bands depended upon the degree of musical ability of the performer rather than on some commercial gimmick of style and dress. From that bygone high plateau still echoes the solid Count Basie's "One O'Clock Jump;" Glenn Miller's "Tuxedo Junction;" Benny Goodman playing "Tiger Rag" at his Carnegie Hall concert; the lyrical clarinet of Artie Shaw playing "Begin the Beguine;" Ziggy Elman ripping off his unique trumpet solo in "And the Angels Sing." The New Orleans Dixieland tradition was kept alive by Bob Crosby's Bob Cats while Duke Ellington towered above everyone on a plateau all his own. (Ellington, incidentally, now in his 70's, is still up there and constantly reaching for loftier musical heights. As this is being written, Ellington, under the auspices of the State Department, is making a highly successful concert tour of Russia.)

Some tunes of the 1930's will forever be associated with certain bands: "Moonlight Serenade" with Glenn Miller, "I Can't Get Started With You" with Bunny Berigan, "Gettin' Sentimental Over You" with Tommy Dorsey, "Woodchoppers Ball" with Woody Herman, "Ciribiribin" with Harry James, "When It's Sleepy Time Down South" with Louis Armstrong, "Sunrise Serenade" with Frankie Carl, "I've Got a Right to Sing the Blues" with Jack Teagarden.

The dedicated music fan of the big band days could tune in a radio music program and identify, just by listening, not only the band that was playing, but the jazz soloists and all the sidemen, plus the singer. The hep cats of the day conversed in their own jive talk. An "alligator" was a swing fan, a "canary" a girl vocalist. One who did not understand swing was square, but one inspired by the music was "in the groove" and "out of this world." One did not smoke grass or pot in those days; he had a "stick of tea." And the uncomplimentary terms reserved for the commercial bands that did not swing were "corn," "rickyticky," "Mickey Mouse," "schmaltz," or "sweet."

A number of successful big bands did not swing; they played a contrived, uninspired brand of commercial pop that catered to banal and mediocre tastes— of which there has always been plenty in the pop music scene. These bands used such devices as singing song titles, rippling or bubbling rhythm and ticktock sounds. In this category were bands such as Blue Barron, Del Courtney, Tommy Tucker, Jan Garber, Kay Kyser, Sammy Kaye, and Shep Fields.

Each band, whether it swung or not, had its own sound and personality. Much depended upon the leader. Some leaders inspired their men and were fun to work for; others were temperamental, hard to get along with or irresponsible. Some bands were constantly bored while others projected an aura of excitement. A good example of contrasting leaders were the Dorsey Brothers. Tommy, not the easiest band leader to work for, was a strict disciplinarian. His group functioned like a tight, smooth machine. His brother, Jimmy, on the other hand, was an easy-going, good-natured character who ran a relaxed, fun-loving band.

There was no thrill to compare with that of hearing live and close a solid, top performing big band of that day. George T. Simon, music critic for the magazine *Metronome* expressed it well in his book, *The Big Bands:*

". . . . To stand in front of one of your favorite swing bands *watching* its musicians make the sounds you'd been *hearing* over the air and on records, and most of all, hearing it in all its roaring purity—with the trumpets and trombones blasting away right at you and the saxes supporting them and the rhythm section letting loose with those clear, crisp, swinging beats—it all added up to one of the real thrills in life.

"There's nothing to match it today. The whining electrified guitars and the flabby-sounding electric basses of the sixties have power, all right—they can virtually steamroller you. But hearing big bands in person was completely different. They didn't knock you down and flatten you out and leave you lying there, a helpless victim of sodden, sullen, mechanized musical mayhem. Instead they swung freely and joyously. And as they swung, they lifted you high in the air with them, filling you with an exhilarated sense of friendly well-being; you joined them, emotionally and musically, as partners in on one of the happiest, most thrilling rapports ever established between the givers and takers of music."

There were, of course, the song writers who created the melodies and lyrics. Best known composers of songs we still sing and play today were George and Ira Gershwin, Cole Porter and Irving Berlin. But there were lesser known song writers such as Ruth Lowe who composed the most touching ballad of the war years, "I'll Never Smile Again."

In 1936, the big hits of the year were "All My Eggs

in One Basket," "Alone," "It's a Sin to Tell a Lie,"
"Lights Out," "Moon over Miami," "Chapel in the
Moonlight," "Did I Remember?," "Is it True What
They Say About Dixie?," "On the Beach at Bali Bali,"
"Pennies from Heaven," "Red Sails in the Sunset,"
"The Way You Look Tonight," "When Did You Leave
Heaven?," "When I'm With You," and probably the
biggest hit of the year, the novelty tune, "The Music
Goes 'Round and 'Round."

In 1937, the top tunes were "Boo Hoo," "Chapel
in the Moonlight," "Harbor Lights," "It Looks Like
Rain," "Little Old Lady," "Moonlight and Shadows,"
"My Cabin of Dreams," "Once in a While," "Sailboat
in the Moonlight," "September in the Rain," "So Rare,"
"That Old Feeling," "Vieni Vieni," "When My Dream-
boat Comes Home," "You Can't Stop Me from Dream-
ing."

The following year, 1938, saw a tune high on the
hit polls that dated back to the early 1900's: "Alexan-
der's Ragtime Band," because a popular movie was
based on the tune. Other top songs were "A-Tisket,
A-Tasket," "Bei Mir Bist Du Schön" (the big hit identi-
fied with the Andrews Sisters), "Cathedral in the
Pines," "Heigh-Ho" (from the Walt Disney success,
Snow White and the Seven Dwarfs), "I've Got a
Pocket Full of Dreams" (Bing Crosby's big hit), "Love
Walked In," "Music, Maestro, Please!," "My Reverie,"
"Rosalie," "Says my Heart," "Thanks for the Memory"
(which became Bob Hope's theme melody), "There's
A Gold Mine in the Sky," "Ti-Pi-Tin," "Whistle While
You Work" (another hit from *Snow White*).

In 1939, Bennie Goodman's band featuring the
trumpet work of Ziggy Elman scored high with "And

the Angels Sing." Other big tunes of the year were "Beer Barrel Polka," "Deep in a Dream," "Deep Purple," "Jeepers Creepers," "Man with the Mandolin," "Moon Love," "My Prayer," "Over The Rainbow," "Penny Serenade," "Three Little Fishes," "Umbrella Man," "Wishing," and "You Must Have Been a Beautiful Baby."

The start of a new decade, 1940, heard the following top pop melodies: "Blueberry Hill," "Careless," "Ferryboat Serenade," "God Bless America" (identified with Kate Smith), "I'll Never Smile Again," "In an Old Dutch Garden," "Indian Summer," "Make Believe Island," "Oh Johnny," "Only Forever," "Playmates," "Scatterbrain," "South of the Border," "When You Wish Upon a Star," and "Woodpecker Song."

Who sang the songs while America listened? Well, there were Patty, Maxine and Laverne, the Andrews Sisters who recorded "Rum and Coca Cola," "Apple Blossom Time," "Bei Mir Bist Du Schön," among many other hits of the day. The Ink Spots, with their style of high falsetto lead and "talking" choruses were singing, "If I Didn't Care," while the Mills brothers who have been around since the 1920's and are still going strong today were vying with the Pied Pipers for top popularity ratings in the groups.

Billie Holiday sang the blues. And if that were not enough there were such superb girl singers as "Liltin'" Martha Tilton, Helen O'Connell, Peggy Lee, Helen Forrest, Mildred Bailey, Marion Hutton, Jo Stafford, Helen Ward, and above all, Ella Fitzgerald (still a consistent winner in polls of top female jazz singers).

But at the head of all the lists was a slender

young male vocalist of the Tommy Dorsey band—
Frank Sinatra. He was the cause of near riots among
the screaming, fainting mobs of bobby soxers. It was,
perhaps, symbolic that in the middle 1950's, near the
close of their careers in popular music, the Dorsey
Brothers introduced another new singer on their TV
show—a youngster named Elvis Presley. Less than
two years later, both the Dorsey brothers were dead.
An era had ended, and the new music of Elvis Presley
was taking over.

What happened to the big bands—what made
them go out of style after World War II? Many
factors were involved. These big bands had depended
upon long trips between one night stands to reach
their audiences. It was not unusual for a band to play
a dance and then travel 500 miles to the following
night's engagement. The musicians on the road virtually lived in busses and automobiles. When the war
started, travel was restricted. Gasoline and tires were
hard to come by. Automobiles and busses wore out
and could not be replaced. So the bands were no
longer able to appear before their audiences in scattered areas of the nation. Too, the draft thinned their
ranks as musicians went off to war, many, like Glenn
Miller, never to come back. The night club and dance
hall business was seriously hurt by a twenty percent
amusement tax levied by the government as a wartime
measure but retained for many years after the war
ended. Perhaps more fundamental than any of these
causes is the basic fickleness of the pop music audience. The big band sound had had its day. Now the
fans were restlessly seeking something new.

A few of the large bands have survived successfully right to the present time and are still popular. There are Count Basie, Duke Ellington, Woody Herman and Harry James; and Stan Kenton still books engagements. But what a handful they are compared to the 300 bands that were playing in the late 1930's!

The recordings of that remarkable episode in American popular music are constantly being reissued and reinterpreted. On Capital ST 2992 one can hear *Artie Shaw Re-creates His Great '38 Band,* a marvelous, smooth-flowing collection of that band's top hits: "Lover Come Back to Me," "Begin the Beguine," "Nightmare," and others. Walt Levinsky interprets Shaw's clarinet style to perfection on the album. On RCA Victor's LSP-2698, *Together Again,* Benny Goodman reassembles his original quartet—Teddy Wilson on piano, Lionel Hampton on vibes, Gene Krupa on drums and Goodman on clarinet—and proves they have lost none of their fire in the intervening thirty years. An even more recent album is *Benny Goodman Today* released by London records, recorded live in Stockholm.

Far from having to search for recordings of the big band years, one can find albums in every record store and new ones are constantly being reissued, testifying to the enduring quality of that musical era.

There is one drawback to listening today to this fine music of the big band age. It is out of the context of its own time and place. The music is as good as ever, but as we listen, something is missing—we should be reading in the newspaper about the latest escapades of Bonnie and Clyde and John Dillinger, and the latest flagpole sitting record and the marathon dance contests and the WPA projects and CCC camps.

Franklin D. Roosevelt should be president and Joe Louis the heavyweight champion of the world. It should be the tail end of a simpler, quieter rural America of small towns and fading innocence. And we'd be marching off to what might have been America's last patriotic war. Because this was the kind of music the young generation dug back then, a time that has gone forever leaving with us its songs as its most living reminder.

Louis "Satchmo" Armstrong—*photo, courtesy of International Musician*

9 The Blues Gets Rhythm and Soul

As the Mississippi river flows south below Memphis, Tennessee, down through Baton Rouge, Louisiana, it winds through rich, alluvian bottom lands. This is the heart of cotton country in the South, believed by many to be the birthplace of the blues. This original "country blues," a kind of Negro folk singing that has been described as "bitterly impassioned" and "fiercely introspective," is voiced by blues singers like John Lee Hooker, Lightning Hopkins, Charlie Patton, Son House, Robert Johnson, Bukka White, Muddy Waters, all blues singers of the most honest and heartfelt kind.

Country blues singers usually start out as soloists, providing their own accompaniment on the guitar. They perform in a loose, rambling style. Often their songs are spaced with a line of spoken patter which might serve as an introduction to the song proper, or simply as a fill-in to keep the mood going while the performer "fools around" with his guitar, retuning strings and striking random chords. This spoken patter, characteristic of many country blues singers, has an extemporaneous style that is an integral part of this kind of blues expression.

For the most part, these blues singers earned their living at jobs other than music and sang their blues for relaxation and enjoyment, perhaps picking

up a few dollars at social functions. Some performers, however, who were handicapped, turned to music
as their only source of livelihood. They sang in bars
and on street corners for tips. The nature of this kind
of performing required that they be constantly on the
move, drifting from street corner to street corner and
from city to city, and in this way they spread their
style of blues singing from country to urban centers.
One of the best known of these early itinerant blues
singers was Blind Lemon Jefferson who was born in
Galveston, Texas, in 1885, and spent most of his life
in the Texas and Louisiana area. He was one of the
first of the early blues singers to be recorded. His
records include "Hangman's Blues," "Rabbit Foot
Blues," "Southern Woman Blues," "Black Snake
Moon," and "The Long, Lonesome Blues."

Perhaps even better known than Blind Lemon
was his pupil, Huddie Ledbetter, better known as
"Leadbelly," who was born in Mooringsport, Louisiana, around 1888. He first became acquainted with
Blind Lemon around 1905 and for a while traveled
with the sightless performer as his guide. Leadbelly
mastered the accordian, harmonica, mandolin, piano
and guitar. He rose to national fame as an authentic
blues singer, recorded for the Library of Congress and
made successful European tours.

While the country blues singers usually sang
their blues alone, sometimes an evening's social func-
tion called for dancing as well as listening, and when
this was the case, the blues singers called on some
friends to help provide a rhythm section, thus forming
a small musical group. From these combinations
came the "spasm" bands and the jug bands employing

such inexpensive and often home-made instruments as jugs, washboards, kazoos and harmonicas. Some of these musicians showed great ingenuity in rigging up washboards with various attachments such as pie plates, cow bells and skillets to expand their rhythmic versatility. In some cases, string bands were formed which included string bass, fiddle and mandolin.

This kind of primitive music-making was heard principally in the black rural communities and in some of the traveling medicine and variety shows which made the circuit of small southern towns.

Meanwhile, in New Orleans, Memphis, up and down the Mississippi, in parts of Texas and later in Chicago, the early jazz bands were including the blues as an important element in their repertoires. It is generally agreed among jazz historians that the earliest group that played music which could be defined as jazz was Buddy Bolden's band which was well known in New Orleans in the late 1890's and early 1900's. During that period music was going through a transition from ragtime to jazz, and it could be debatable which of the two Buddy Bolden played, since we have no recordings of his music. But old timers who heard him described his music as an early, rough form of jazz, and they all say blues made up a good portion of what he played. Some observers said that he really got into the dirty, low-down blues at his dances after midnight, at which time the more respectable people went home.

While Buddy Bolden will forever remain something of a shadowy legend in jazz annals, the remarkable Ferdinand "Jelly Roll" Morton left behind concrete evidence of his genius in the form of recordings and written compositions, many of them preserved in the Library of Congress. Jelly Roll, who was not exactly a shy man (he had a diamond set in a front tooth), claimed that he invented jazz. After listening to some of his exquisite compositions, "Wolverine Blues," "King Porter Stomp," "The Original Jelly Roll Blues," "Sidewalk Blues," and "The Pearls," one is tempted to agree with him. Of course, he didn't actually invent jazz; no one person did; it was an outgrowth of many forms of music: marches, ragtime, spirituals, blues—but Jelly Roll, who first played in the red light districts of New Orleans in the early 1900's, certainly elevated jazz from some of its cruder beginnings and gave us a legacy of compositions that will be played as long as jazz endures. His approach to the blues expression was inventive and varied, departing from the traditional concept. In fact, if one tried to use a yardstick of strict definition, some of Jelly Roll's "blues" compositions might not even fall within that boundary except in overall mood and tone. Certainly Jelly Roll did not confine himself to the twelve-bar, tonic, sub-dominant, dominant standard blues form.

Not only Jelly Roll, but all the early classic jazz musicians—Sidney Bechet, Kid Ory, King Oliver—played the blues. And this is true down to modern jazz performers like Charlie Parker and Miles Davis. They are all masters of the blues form. Many of Duke Ellington's monumental arrangements revolve around the blues pattern, while the famous "jump" tunes of the big band era, "One O'Clock Jump," "Woodchopper's Ball" and "In the Mood," are simply the blues chord progressions played in swinging, jitterbug-tempo "riffs" or phrases.

Trombonist Jack Teagarden was an outstanding white jazz musician who played the blues as eloquently as black jazz artists. And of course, the greatest of all the jazz musicians, Louis "Satchmo" Armstrong, often turned his musical genius to expressing the blues.

In tracing the evolution of blues styles down to today's popular rhythm 'n' blues and soul, blues history can be broken down into four general periods. First, was the early country blues, already discussed in Chapter 5. Then came a period in the 1920's called the "classic" city blues during which time recordings were made by the great women blues singers like Bessie Smith. In the 1930's and 1940's there developed the "urban blues" which was played by larger bands with a more pronounced rhythmic beat until the addition of electrically amplified guitars led it to the rhythm 'n' blues style. Finally, we have soul which is the blues strongly flavored with a jazz beat and gospel chords and emotion. Ray Charles towers as the outstanding exponent of soul.

During the early decades of this century, the authentic forms of native American music were considered disreputable. Recording companies avoided jazz, white hillbilly and black blues as if they might contaminate the Victrolas of America. Jazz music? That was something played in houses of ill repute. Hillbilly? Who but uneducated backwoods country hicks wanted to hear that. And blues? Well, that was "nigger music."

So, the recording companies maintained their respectability and decorum by producing records of European style music hall numbers, marches and symphonic works with a few novelty releases thrown in. But following World War I, jazz began spreading rapidly and gained in popularity, and in 1917, the Victor Recording Company stuck its neck out and recorded the Original Dixieland Jazz Band. The records sold well.

In 1920, the Okeh Record Company of New York set a milestone in the history of popular music when it made the first commercial recording of a Negro blues singer, Mamie Smith. Her "Crazy Blues" record sold 8,000 copies a week, which was not bad for that time. It convinced the record companies that they had tapped a new market—the Negro audience. Thus was developed a new branch of the recording field called "race records" since they were produced specifically for the Negro race.

About the same time, recording companies were also discovering that hillbilly records could ring the cash register. "It Ain't Gonna Rain No Mo'," recorded by Wendell Hall, became Victor's top hit of 1923.

The success of these early blues and hillbilly records inspired record companies to go on recording safaris into the rural poverty belt of the Appalachian hillbilly country and through the Negro communities in the South in search of authentic talent. They carried recording equipment in trucks and would stop in a town, rent a couple of vacant rooms in a store building, convert them into a makeshift recording studio and round up local talent for recording sessions. They also ventured into the Negro ghettos of such large cities as Atlanta, Dallas, Houston, Memphis, Kansas City, St. Louis and Chicago. It was these wandering units that "discovered" such hillbilly immortals as the Carter Family and Jimmie Rodgers and gave them to the world.

The 1920's decade was a "golden age" of the blues. This classic period saw blues and jazz mingled to produce some immortal artistic achievements of the highest quality. For an all too brief time such splendid Negro women blues singers as Ma Rainey, Ida Cox, Memphis Minnie, Merline Johnson, Victoria Spiney and Lil Green moaned and wailed their blues which were frozen in time by the cutting needles of the recording equipment and released for the world to hear over and over for as long as people care to listen. There were a number of fine blues singers named "Smith"—Mamie, Bessie, Laura, Trixie and Clara, none of them related, but all of them top blues shouters and moaners. Later, the city blues was to develop a driving, amplified beat and branch off from its association with jazz to become rhythm'n'blues.

The classic period produced the greatest woman blues singer of all times, Bessie Smith. In my book on the history of jazz, *Cool, Hot and Blue,* I described Bessie Smith and her career as follows:

"Race records immortalized the songs of the most famous woman blues singer in jazz history, the incomparable Bessie Smith. Bessie was a lady with a big body, a big voice and a big heart who lived the blues she sang. She was born of a very poor family in Chattanooga, Tennessee, on April 17, 1894. She learned how to sing the blues from Ma Rainey. In the 1920's, Bessie Smith enjoyed periods of great prosperity, earning as much as two thousand dollars a week. When she made a record, lines a block long would form in Negro neighborhoods outside the stores that sold her recordings. She was accompanied on these records by some of the greatest jazz musicians—Louis Armstrong, clarinettist Buster Bailey, pianist James P.

Johnson and the Fletcher Henderson band. She had a deep, poignant voice and sang with tremendous feeling and power. But she drank too much and threw her money away like a child in a candy store. She was generous to a fault."

During that time in the 1920's, Bessie Smith was Columbia Record's most popular recording star. In 1924, more than two million copies of her records were sold. It is said that at one time she alone saved the recording company from bankruptcy. She is constantly being "re-discovered" by blues lovers. A most complete selection of her records is contained in the Columbia four-album set of the *Bessie Smith Story*. Volume one (Columbia CL 855) is particularly valuable because on many of her songs Bessie is accompanied by Louis Armstrong. Other Bessie Smith reissues on LP albums have recently been released.

There were no such things as stereo or high fidelity record players or tape decks back in the days when Bessie Smith sang. Her records were heavy 78 rpm singles of about three minutes playing time on each side that would break as easily as a dinner plate if dropped. To listen to them, you hand cranked your Victrola until the spring motor was wound tightly, put in a fresh steel needle (good for four or five records after which it had to be replaced again), placed the heavy arm on the spinning disk, and listened to the tinny, low-fi reproduction that covered only a narrow range of the sound spectrum. When the music lost its pitch and slowed down and the singer's voice dropped from a soprano to a basso profundo, it was time to give the wind-up mechanism some fresh turns on the crank. But despite these primitive record machines, it was a great musical age. The greatness

of the music transcended the limitations of the recording equipment.

All over the country during the period of the Jazz
Age, people were cranking up their phonographs and
listening to country blues singers like Barbecue Bob,
Peg Leg Howell, Blind Willie Johnson, Lillian Glinn,
Pink Anderson, Blind Willie McTell, Bobby Cadillac
and Aaron T-Bone Walker who had been recorded by
the mobile recording units roaming the South.

A branch of the blues style adopted by piano
players and characterized by a rolling, eight-to-the-bar
bass, came to be known as "boogie-woogie." Jimmy
Yancey, Albert Ammons and Clarence "Pine Top"
Smith were the foremost exponents of this style of
rhythmic blues. It was very popular at the "rent parties" which were prevalent in the Negro sections of
the large cities in the 1920's and 1930's. The purpose
of the parties (which might go on all week-end) was,
as the name implies, to raise the month's rent for the
host. Refreshments were served, music was furnished
by alternating pianists who dropped in, and the hat
was passed for contributions toward paying the rent.
In his book, *Blues People,* LeRoi Jones says, "The
boogie pianist achieved a special social status, playing at the various Chittlin' Struts, Gumbo Suppers,
Fish Fries, Egg Nog Parties. His services were much
sought after, and he could gain entrance to all these
'pay parties' without being expected to pay."

White audiences caught up to the boogie-woogie
style in the mid and late 1930's when some of the big
bands popularized it with arrangements of tunes like,
"Beat Me Daddy, Eight to the Bar," "Boogie Woogie
Bugle Boy," "Bumble Boogie," and others.

The classic age of the blues drew to a close with

the end of the Jazz Age as the bottom fell out of the
stock market in 1929 and The Great Depression began. The next phase in blues development centered
around four principal cities: Chicago, Detroit, Kansas
City and Memphis and in the Southwest dance terri-
tory, especially the Texas-Oklahoma area. It was the
blues which Negro bands played in these sections
that evolved into urban rhythm'n'blues which then
helped give birth to rock'n'roll and a revolution in
America's popular music.

When the depression hit, record sales fell drasti-
cally. In 1932, only six million records were sold as
compared to 104 million just five years before in
1927. To cope with the dismal economy, Victor put
out a cheaper subsidiary line, Bluebird, which carried
race and hillbilly artists. In 1934, the Decca Record
Company was organized and put their records on the
market for 35¢ each instead of the standard 75¢ being
charged by the older record companies. Decca became
an immediate success and the price war that resulted
forced other companies to lower the prices of their
first line records. Thus, the record companies struggled through the depression years, but it was not
until the Long Play, high fidelity albums and 45 rpm
singles appeared on the scene in the late 1940's that
the recording industry was once again to feel the
glow of success.

The migration of Negro blues from the delta
country of Mississippi, the rural areas of Texas, the
old deep South states of Georgia and Alabama to
cities further north parallels the changes that were
coming to the black life and thinking in America.
World War I opened the first doors to industrial

jobs and improved living conditions of rural Negroes who started a migration to urban centers that has continued to today. As black people struggled both to find a place in the mainstream of American life and an identity of their own in a predominantly white society, the music that is more Negro than any other kind—the blues—played a role of large cultural importance to them. The Negro's first heroes were in the fields of sports and music. (His hero-prototypes in politics, literature, education and law were to come later.) There were two trap doors out of the dark economic cellar in which he was trapped: sports and music. If he had a degree of musical talent he was one step ahead of the game. It could bring him anything from additional part-time earnings to a possible career of importance. It certainly beat shining shoes. However, of more importance than these considerations, practical as they are to the Negro community at large, the blues has consistently been linked to the warp and woof of their culture. It has provided the black man the rhythm and mood for his dances, the pivot of his social and recreational life, the expression of his feelings. It has been *his* music, something white society could neither dilute nor deprive him of. It has also provided him, when he wished, with a shield of privacy around a cultural expression uniquely his own, because white people cannot always understand what he is saying when he gives voice to the blues.

During the period from the mid-1920's to the early 1940's, Negro bands home-based in Kansas City toured the Southwest, ranging down into Negro communities in Texas, Oklahoma, Missouri and Arkansas. These were large bands of eight pieces or more. They were basically swing-dance bands that mingled jazz and blues numbers and could not be defined as strictly "blues" groups. Kansas City in those days of the Pendergast political regime was a wide open town run largely by gangsters. It was a mecca for jazz musicians because many night clubs were using bands. Some of the great Negro bands of that Kansas City era, which became as well known to the white community as to the black, included Bennie Moton, Count Basie, Louis Jordan and Hot Lips Page.

In the 1940's, these larger bands of the swing era began dying out. By that time, the amplified guitar had been introduced on the music scene and as the decibels increased, the size of the bands decreased. Backed up by a powerhouse of amplification, the single guitar could provide a big, solid sound that equaled the volume of several unamplified instruments. The bands touring the Southwest became smaller, but louder, put more emphasis on rhythm and confined their repertoire almost exclusively to blues numbers. Brass instruments—trumpets and trombones—were rarely seen any more in these smaller groups. They concentrated on the amplified guitar, a solo blues singer whose voice was also amplified via the microphone and public address system, and the tenor or alto saxophone. The acendency of the saxophone in the growing rhythm-and-blues field and the increasing lack of interest in other traditional jazz instruments—clarinet, trumpet and trombone—is interesting. One explanation might be that the saxophone, more than the other instruments mentioned, can be made to wail and moan in the style of a blues singer's voice and can also express rasping, gutty, low-down sounds. But these things go in cycles and there is a trend in some larger blues-flavored rock groups such as Blood, Sweat and Tears to again make use of the traditional jazz instruments.

Ironically, it was with Negro audiences that the country blues fell into disfavor. Since a large portion of the Negro population had migrated to cities and was employed in offices, automobile factories, steel mills and retail stores it made little sense to sing about the old country blues subject material of farm-life, picking cotton, and share-cropping. Besides, the country blues symbolized a time of bitterness and degradation that was an unpleasant memory to many Negroes. Blues singer "Big" Bill Hill explained that the blues "has something to do with that bastard part of life most black people want to forget." Much of the black audience prefers soul which expresses strongly the gospel, jazz influence. And the driving sound of rhythm'n'blues which grew up with the urban Negroes was for many a more sincere form of communication.

But in the 1950's, white audiences discovered country blues and there has been a continuing revival of interest in these basic blues roots ever since. Rock, no matter in which direction it strays—hard rock, acid rock, psychedelic rock, folk-rock—has its first source of energy in the blues. Eric Clapton, a white English blues guitarist, says that rock must constantly return to the blues to get its battery recharged.

Blues singer B. B. King (Riley B. King), born in Ita Bena, Mississippi, September 16, 1925, strongly influenced by T-Bone Walker and the heartfelt mood of country blues, struggled for twenty years, roaming the South with his band, barely surviving. Straight blues, with the northern black audiences, was out; rhythm'n'blues was in. Then these black audiences turned to singers like James Brown and Aretha Franklin who were strong on church-oriented soul music. In 1968, King was booked into the Fillmore West. He'd played there in 1963 to a 95 percent black audience that had given him a luke-warm reception. This time his audience was 95 percent white and they gave him a standing ovation. That night B. B. King had grabbed the tail of a comet that was on a glory path. He has become the biggest name in the blues field with hits like "Cash Box" and "Record World" and a Grammy Award or "The Thrill is Gone." Much of his audience is still the audience of young whites who are busy learning all about the blues.

There is nothing faked about King's "root" feeling for country blues. He chopped cotton and rode mules as a kid in Mississippi, and sang spirituals at church, but idolized his uncle, Booker T. Washington White, and Blind Lemon Jefferson. He still carries tapes of their records around with him wherever he goes. The top jazz guitarist, Django Reinhardt, was B.B.'s instrumental idol. There is an irony to all his success, however. He has never been asked to appear at a black college. His great hope is that Negroes will become unashamed of the blues—their own music. (He is referring to basic country blues.)

Hot on B.B.'s success trail in the blues revival is his half brother, Albert King. Like B.B., he plays guitar left-handedly with the strings upside down for no real reason except that's how he learned to play it. Like his half brother, he's dug the gutty blues out of the sun-baked cotton fields and mud bayous, but be-

yond that he has a style of his own. Success began
to smile on this 250-pound former bulldozer driver
from the night he was booked into the Fillmore West
in San Francisco in 1968 on the same bill with Big
Brother and the Holding Company where they played
to a packed house. Among his top selling records
have been "Laundromat Blues" and "I've Been Gone
Too Long."

Most of the authentic rural blues singers have
spent the major portion of their lives in humble cir-
cumstances, playing for Negro audiences and perhaps
making a few race records. The word "rediscovery"
symbolizes the turning point in their careers, usually
in the late 1960's when they have come to the attention of the blues revival among white intellectuals.
The authentic blues has become a vital, powerful
American folk music. Son House (Eddie James House,
Jr.) played at levee camps and country dances in
Mississippi in the 1920's and 1930's, but had given
music up completely by 1960. Then, in 1964, he was
"rediscovered," performed for the Philadelphia Folk
Festival in August of that year and began a whole
new career, this time playing for predominantly white
audiences.

Sleepy John Estes, born in Tennessee in 1904,
was totally blind when he was rediscovered in 1962.
Music critic Pete Welding says about Sleepy John
Estes, "There is a strong feeling of intense anguish
and inconsolate, piercing sorrow in Estes' singing."
This aptly describes the emotions prevalent in the
troubled sadness heard in the country blues style.

Muddy Waters has been called the "father figure" of the blues revival movement, while John Lee

Hooker, born in Clarksdale, Mississippi, is described by jazz writer Marshall Stearns as, "one of the few truly authentic exponents of archaic guitar style, a style which may well trace back to Civil War days."

One of the folk-legendary figures in rural blues is William Lee Conley Broonzy, better known as Big Bill Broonzy, who had one of the earthiest, most powerful styles of traditional blues singing. His mother, born in slavery, lived to the age of 102 and died just a year before Big Bill's death in Chicago in 1958. His autobiography, *Bill Bill Blues*, told to Belgian jazz writer, Yannick Bruynoghe, was published by Grove Press in 1957 and would make interesting reading to the student of rural blues singers.

Sam "Lightnin'" Hopkins is another country blues singer who reappeared on the music scene by the magic touchstone of "rediscovery." He learned to sing the blues listening to Blind Lemon Jefferson, then moved from his farm in Centerville, Texas, to Houston where he roamed the streets, playing for small sums, until he was rediscovered. Then he found himself in New York, performing for white blues fans at clubs like the Village Gate.

Moving to the field of today's "big-beat" sound of urban blues, two large performing and recording centers are Detroit and Memphis. Detroit's "Motown" sound emphasizes the drums and bass in a heavy, overriding beat. The highly popular "Supremes" are products of Detroit.

The "Memphis sound" seems to place more emphasis on brass and guitar. It is quite appropriate that Memphis should become a hub of blues activity. Memphis was the town where W. C. Handy first gave a name to "the blues" with compositions like "Mr.

Crump" (later renamed "The Memphis Blues"), the "St. Louis Blues" and "Beale Street Blues."

Today's "queen of the Memphis sound" is the five-foot-four package of seductive blues singing, Carla Thomas. Her career got off to a big start with the hit "Cause I love You," and includes other hits such as "When Something is Wrong With My Baby," "Let Me Be Good to You," and "Tramp."

Carla Thomas has recorded duets with Otis Redding who has been called the "king of the Memphis sound." A few of his top selling records are "These Arms of Mine" and "I've Been Loving Too Long," and he won a Grammy Award with "Dock of the Bay." Redding was killed in a plane crash in Wisconsin in December of 1967, but his records continue to influence the rhythm and blues field.

Instrumentalists of the Memphis sound are Booker T. and the MG's. (Booker T. Jones, who holds a bachelor's degree in applied music from the University of Indiana, is the leader of the group. "MG" is an abbreviation for the Memphis Group.) This rhythm'n'blues group has won a *Billboard* poll as the top instrumental combo.

The Memphis sound has its soul or gospel singers, too, for soul along with country blues and rock'n'-roll all blend to produce the Memphis sound which *Billboard* magazine has called "the most exciting musical product of our time." Foremost among the Memphis gospel singers is a group called the Staple Singers. They are not natives of Memphis, but have been attracted to this blues mecca on the banks of the sprawling, muddy Mississippi by the recording facilities and the surging blues-soul climate.

Tops among today's female singers in the blues-soul category is Aretha Franklin. Born right in the heart of it all—where it's at—Memphis, Tennessee, in 1942, she had an early first-hand exposure to church choir singing in the New Bethel Baptist Church where her father was pastor. She traveled the gospel circuit until she was 18, then switched to secular music and began recording for Columbia Records in 1960. Moving with easy facility from gospel to blues to current pop songs, she has produced such hit albums as, *Aretha, The Electrifying Aretha Franklin, Unforgettable,* and *Yeah!*

Any discussion of jazz-blues-rhythm'n'blues-gospel and soul has to come finally to rest on Ray Charles, for he is the man who has put it all together better than anyone else. Perhaps he has felt it more deeply than anyone else: the sadness, the jazz, the beat. He was blind at six, orphaned at fifteen, became a narcotics addict by the time he was sixteen, but emerged from the dark world of drugs by his own strength of character and will-power when he was thirty-two. When he sings about trouble and sorrow and soul-weariness, Lord, he knows. He's been there. Not all rhythm'n'blues performers are respected by jazz musicians, but Ray Charles is because he swings with the best of them. Not all soul singers are popular with the general public, but Ray Charles is because he has that uncanny ability to choose the kind of material the public will like and deliver it with a warmth and poignancy that touches a responsive chord in everyone. In his day, Al Jolsen had it, and Bing Crosby had it, and Frank Sinatra had it with the pop music crowd of the times and it carried over into other times. If there is a performer around today whose work will live beyond the immediate pop fads of rhythm'n'blues, soul and rock, it probably is Ray Charles.

On his twenty-fifth anniversary in show business, in February, 1971, Ray Charles was honored by the world premiere performances of Quincy Jones' *Black Requiem* with the Houston Symphony in Houston, Texas. The composition was dedicated to Ray Charles and he was the featured performer. "He grunts and sings and plays it," the award-winning composer-conductor said. "Nobody else could handle it."

Jones described his work as "a prayer for the dead and an expression of hope for the living. My Catholic mother will never forgive me, but it's high mass transplanted to the Baptist Church, the kind that was across the street from our house, that had electric guitars and trombones and it really smoked."

The *Black Requiem* is a seven-art work for orchestra, 60-voice chorus, and "one man that's as much musician as Ray Charles."

The requiem is a musical statement of the black experience in America: the slavery, confusion after emancipation, passive resistance, rhetoric of the ghetto and a riot built right into it. The black slave chants, religious songs, African rhythms and swinging modern jazz improvisations are all combined and mingled with symphonic music in a jazz-oriented idiom.

The requiem was performed twice in Houston, first at the predominantly Negro college, Prairie View, and then in downtown Houston's Jones Hall. Charles received a "roaring, standing ovation," according to Houston *Post* critic, Carl Cunningham.

There is an interesting footnote to the performance of this powerful, emotionally-charged work of
music. A week after its performance, Prairie View
was the scene of a massive riot and burning of build-
ings. The age-old question that philosophers and psy-
chologists have pondered since Plato's time is again
raised—how much effect does music have on human
conduct for good or evil?

America's popular music has undergone drastic
changes since the turn of the century. A citizen of the
year 1900, transported suddenly to a psychedelic hard
rock concert with 100 decibel amplifiers and a light
show would scarcely believe he was on the same
planet. Only one thing he might recognize, one musical form that has constantly remained like a common
denominator through the mutations of pop music—
that good, old standard twelve-bar blues. The inevitable tonic, sub-dominant, dominant chord progression.
It has virtually become the seminal archetype of
America's pop music trends. It was here when jazz
was king, it provided swing its most reliable refer-
ence, bop and progressive fell back on it time and
again, rhythm'n'blues is totally immersed in it, and
rock'n'roll was born and survives because of it. And
it will no doubt be around long after today's musical
fads have become moldy history. It is expressed most
honestly and artistically when it falls into the hands
of jazz musicians and the original country blues singers who thought it up. It becomes gimmicky and dis-
torted by hard rock groups. But where would they be
without it?

Janis Joplin was influenced by Bessie Smith records to pursue a musical career. The Rolling Stones,

the Beatles and Bob Dylan all need the blues like a wounded hemophiliac needs constant blood transfusions. Where would the Rolling Stones be without Muddy Waters? Mike Bloomfield's Electric Flag; Canned Heat; the Cream; Johnny Winter; the Grateful Dead; Sir Douglas Quintet; Blood, Sweat and Tears and Ten Years After all use the blues form. Jimi Hendrix lived and died in a musical world colored by the blues.

Muddy Waters, a true bluesman, has shown them the path. If you want to hear him, find his album, *Heavy Heads* on the Chess label 1522.

One of the unresolved debates about the blues is, can white musicians express it as sincerely as black performers? "No," Muddy Waters is quoted in the *Newsweek* article, "Rebirth of the Blues." "There are some beautiful white bands. They can play almost anything. But they didn't go to the Baptist Church like I went. They didn't get that soul down deep in the heart like I have. And they can't deliver the message. They're playing the white folks' blues. I'm playing the real blues."

Contradicting that view, Al Wilson, guitarist with Canned Heat says, "You should judge with your ears, not your eyes. Nobody can listen to Paul Butterfield and say that no white man can sing the blues."

As far as I am concerned, Jack Teagarden settled the argument a long time ago. And Peggy Lee keeps settling it all the time. But it is true that real blues singers and musicians with white faces are scarce.

Jimmie Rodgers—*RCA Records photo*

10   Nashville

Nashville has become the big-time Broadway of
the hillbillies. Fame and fortune beckon. The stories
of gold Cadillac convertibles and guitar-shaped swimming pools, symbols of Nashville success, attract each
day a new flood of hopeful song writers and singers.
They come by car, bus, plane, motorcycle, and thumb,
bringing their guitars, western clothes and aspira-
tions. A few make it. Most leave after a year or two,
defeated, but still loyal to country music.

When they bring their hopes to Nashville, they
come to the right place. Nashville is where it's at—
Music City, U.S.A. New York and Hollywood have
been moved over to second fiddles in the great string
band of golden pop. Tin Pan Alley did all right in its
time, but these days it's the music industry down in
Nashville, Tennessee, that is playing the cash register
rag.

More than 52% of all recorded music in the
United States originates in taping sessions in Nashville's recording studios (60% of that is country music). Boil that down to dollars and cents. The total
sales of recorded music in the U.S. in 1970 grossed
one and three quarter billion dollars. If Nashville produced over half of that, the city's recording industry

realized some ⅞ths of a billion dollars. And the total sales of country music records in 1970 amounted to ½ billion dollars.

The saga of this country colossus began in 1925 when the Grand Ole Opry began broadcasting here. This enduring hillbilly radio show was founded by a business partnership of the National Life and Accident Insurance Company and radio station WSM.

The city of Memphis also ranks high as a center of country music activity. While not quite up to Nashville, its pop music industry is highly successful to a degree that bankers find country-pop music a blue-chip investment. Lyman Aldrich, representing the First National Bank in Memphis, got the music leaders of his city together and formed Memphis Music, Inc., an organization whose aim it was to develop Memphis into a music capitol. Bank loans were arranged for projects related to the music and recording activities in that city. As a result, the music industry boomed in Memphis, producing 118 chart records and more than 50 gold million sellers and today brings millions of dollars into that city annually. Such stars as Elvis Presley, Johnny Cash, and Carl Perkins have been "discovered" by Memphis recording studios.

Back in the early days of radio, when the Grand Ole Opry was an infant, there were no recording studios or music publishers in Nashville. Country musicians came out of the hills in Model T Fords and on mules just to perform on the radio without expecting to make any money out of it. Today, there are over 400 music publishers who either have their home offices in Nashville or have a representative office in the city. The total of major and minor recording studios is more than 40. Over a dozen of these are large studios which boast the most up-to-date equipment and sound engineers. Over 300 record labels spring from this music city. Studios include Athena Studios, Bradley's Barn, Cedarwood Sound Studios, Monument Recording Studios, Music City Recorders, Nugget Studios, RCA, Spar Recording Studios, Columbia, DBM Studios, Globe Recording Studios, Gower and Moore Studios, Starday-King, Varsity Sound Studios, Woodland Sound Studios, Faron Young Studios, Mercury Studios and recently those of Buzz Cason, Bobby Russell and Danny Davis.

There are a spate of other enterprises related to the business of making records. Sleeve manufacturers and a catalog service are located here. Also, there are 7 jingle and commercial spot firms, 11 motion picture producers and 9 public relations and promotion agencies for the music business. There are also 6 pressing and plating plants, 5 record distributors, 2 rack jobbers, 13 design and artwork firms specifically serving the music and record field, 5 direct mail houses, 4 tape duplication businesses and 13 photography firms that deal almost entirely with music promotion.

As for the people who make the music—well, some 400 performers and over 900 song writers live in Nashville. The local chapter of the American Federation of Musicians has approximately 1700 members. The American Federation of Television and Radio Artists' local chapter has nearly 700 members. The Nashville Songwriters Association has 400 members, while the Country Music Association, an international organization with headquarters in Nashville, has a total membership of close to three thousand.

(The figures we quote in this chapter are furnished by the CMA, Country Music Association, Inc.)

Nashville's first recording studio was built shortly
after World War II by Owen Bradley in a quonset hut.
He chose for its location a section of the city where a
number of large, old-fashioned homes bordered a business and industrial district. Today this section is
known as Music Row. It is located between Division
Street on the north, 16th Avenue South on the east,
21st Avenue South on the west and Grand Street on
the south.

A monument to country music and its greatest
luminaries is the Country Music Hall of Fame and
Museum built at a cost of nearly a million dollars
which was raised by the music industry from public
and private sources. It is a beautiful, ultra-modern
building which is both a tourist attraction and a museum of country music lore. Here, the visitor can see
historical paraphernalia of the country music world
such as wearing apparel (Jimmie Rodgers' brakeman's
clothing for example), instruments, and other me-
mentos, plus a film on the history of country music.
The primary attraction is, of course, the plaques
which bear the likenesses, names and brief information about those accorded the highest tribute the country music field can offer. The names of some to receive
this distinctive honor include Jimmie Rodgers, Fred
Rose, Hank Williams, Roy Acuff, Tex Ritter, Ernest
Tubb, Uncle Dave Macon, George D. Hay, Eddy Arnold, James Denny, Red Foley, Jim Reeves, J. L.
Frank, Steve Sholes and the Carter family. More, of
course, are being added. The building also houses a
library and media center affiliated with the joint uni-

versity library systems of Vanderbilt, Peabody, and Scarritt Universities, and was completed at a cost of a quarter of a million dollars.

The CMA—Country Music Association, Inc.—is an organization formed by businessmen in various fields related to the country music industry whose purpose is the "preservation, advancement and promotion of country music as a distinct and unique part of the American heritage." (Quoted from CMA's information paper.)

Looking away from Nashville for a moment, let us get a perspective of the tremendous pop success of country-western on a national scale. According to a 1971 CMA radio survey, approximately 700 radio stations in the United States and Canada broadcast country music on a full time basis. In addition, 1575 stations use some country music along with other categories. So, we have one out of every three radio stations on the air broadcasting country music sound at one time or another during the day and night. One out of eight stations air country music continuously.

In the field of national television programs, Glen Campbell's show on the CBS-TV network has done well, while the Johnny Cash Show has had a three-season run as has "Hee Haw." Another development in the TV area is the syndicated show, half-hour and hour long color productions which are used by individual stations all over the nation and feature such country stars as Porter Wagoner, Bill Anderson, Billy Walker, Marty Robbins, Kitty Wells, Johnny Wright, Wilburn Brothers, Buck Owens, Jim Ed Brown, Hugh X. Lewis, plus the Stoneman Family Show, the Homesteaders, and Billy Edd Wheeler.

Some country singers such as Loretta Lynn are also sampling the gravy from the lucrative field of TV commercials.

And, there are the live performances to be considered. Some 50 road shows tour out of Nashville continuously and are booked from coast to coast.

As for the future, Nashville is already eyeing the potential craze for video tape players that is predicted to be the forthcoming entertainment boom. Soon, it is anticipated, Nashville will be packaging video tapes on a gigantic scale, so that country music fans can enjoy their own pick of shows in their homes.

One of the hottest projects currently afoot in Nashville is the $25 million entertainment park, Opryland, U.S.A., which will be the future site of the Grand Ole Opry while at the same time representing other forms of American music, too. It will be located in the eastern suburbs of Nashville, and is being constructed by the National Life and Accident Insurance Company and WSM. Scheduled to open on April 29, 1972, on 369 acres of rolling countryside, this tremendous entertainment complex will contain eight "villages," each depicting a distinctive type of American music. Shows will feature live musical entertainment. It will be a Disneyland designed to immortalize American music. One unit, for example, will be the New Orleans village, highlighting American jazz and blues. The Grand Ole Opry will be located in the Opry Plaza Area and will include a 4,430 seat Opry House and a 300 seat television studio. This portion is scheduled for completion in 1973.

Unquestionably, country music has become one of America's leading industries along with the manufacturing of automobiles, home appliances and "better living through chemistry." It is also a leading export. What is the nature of this new country music, which is as popular in Tokyo, Liverpool, and Berlin as it is in Cut-and-Shoot, Texas, and Smackover, Arkansas?

While today's country music has become smooth and "uptown," there are still two basic elements that distinguish it from the Tin Pan Alley compositions of New York and Hollywood. One is that most country melodies are constructed on very simple chord progressions usually involving no more than three or four of the most basic chords. The other distinguishing feature is that country music lyrics deal in realism, often the seamy, sordid, tragic side of life, and often the treatment reflects a dripping sentimentalism.

While humor and novelty songs from Nashville hit the top charts often these days, the bulk of country hits are still in the "weeper" category. These laments have been called "hurtin' songs," and "crying in your beer" music. As one observer put it, in country ballads the singer is either crying, dying or going someplace. The expression of self-pity is so strong that one must come to the conclusion they satisfy a deep, psychological need in a great many listeners to feel sorry for themselves. This could well be a valid need, considering the woes, heartbreaks and troubles encountered in the average lifetime. Shakespeare's *Hamlet* expressed the burden of living in his soliloquy. Country music interprets his "slings and arrows of outrageous fortune" into the common idiom of the working man and puts it to music he can understand.

Of all the subject matter touched upon in these songs, love—as might be expected—heads the list.

But to the country songwriter, love is a synonym for pure misery. Fickleness, spurned love, rejection, unfaithfulness, all give the singer ample cause to lament. If both parties in the song happen to love equally, then they face insurmountable obstacles, usually in the person of a husband or wife.

A woman's fickle nature is the problem in "She's Looking Good." (What she's looking for is another guy!) "Half a Man" is about all that's left of a poor guy after his girlfriend ditched him. "Four Walls" is what a rejected lover stares at while the object of his or her affection is out having a good time.

In some songs it is the singer who has been untrue, but he or she usually regrets the error of his or her ways and begs for a second chance as in "Try Me One More Time." Sometimes it's too late: "Too Late to Worry, Too Blue to Cry."

Occasionally, the spurned lover finds consolation in the "you'll be sorry one day that you done me wrong" attitude. "Someday You'll Want Me to Want You." But the song goes on to say it will be too late; there are other pebbles on the beach, baby. Parting is such sweet sorrow in "For The Good Times."

There is one genre of "going someplace" songs in which the lover with itchy feet simply packs up and leaves with little conscience and fewer regrets: "By the Time I Get to Phoenix," and "Forget Me."

Now and then, the singer says good riddance: "Thank God and Greyhound, You're Gone!"

The problem of marital infidelity is treated with down-to-earth frankness in many country songs: "Go On Home," "Slipping Around," "Back Street Affair," "One Has My Name and The Other Has My Heart."

Two sides of the eternal triangle readily admit their love is wrong but are powerless to fight it. "Please Help Me, I'm Falling," warns Hank Locklin on one record. "(I Can't Help You) I'm Falling, Too," replies Skeeter Davis helplessly on another recording.

Loneliness is the stock in trade of country Tin Pan Alley. In "Heartbreak Hotel" the word "lonely" appears a total of ten times in the verse and chorus; in "Lonely Street," seven times (not counting the title).

Country music songwriters will tackle almost any subject, no matter how earthy.

Gambling: "Playing Dominoes and Shooting Dice."

Divorce: "Married by the Bible, Divorced by Law."

Drinking: "I'm Going to Tie One on Tonight."

Cigarettes: "Smoke! Smoke! Smoke That Cigarette!"

Poverty in childhood: "Hand-Me-Down Things."

Bootlegging: "White Lightning."

Chewing tobacco and spitting: "Chew Tobacco Rag."

Tuberculosis: "T.B. Blues."

Many country songs carry a simple moral admonition. "Don't Rob Another Man's Castle," meaning don't steal another man's wife. "I did," warns the singer, "and now I've gotten a dose of my own medicine."

Country gospel songs affirm the faith in a personal God: "Take My Hand, Precious Lord," "Let's Talk About Jesus," "I Won't Have to Cross Jordan Alone." The belief in immortality and a future life in heaven is expressed in many songs.

Working people, that is, people who work at
trades, "blue collar" workers, make up a large segment
of the country music audience so it follows that quite
a few songs deal with various kinds of work: steel
workers, track layers, taxi drivers, mine workers. The
job of truck driving has become a prominent classification of country music, taking the place of the once
popular railroad songs. The truck driver hero is a
product of our modern urbanization, the ascendency
of the freeway over steel rails. Examples are songs
such as "Truck Driving Son of a Gun," "Girl on the
Billboard," and "Six Days on the Road."

The tradition of loneliness and sadness in country music is explained by most researchers in terms of
the early rural isolation, the poverty and hard times of
the rural people, the Calvinistic religions they followed and the fact that the early British ballads sung
in the Appalachian mountains were in minor keys.
These factors may clarify the background, but the
continuing widespread popularity of this tragic element despite modern improved standards of living
must be explained in terms of an emotional need to
relate one's personal heartaches to that of the song
and to identify with the sufferer in the song.

Hank Williams, quoted in an article, "Country
Music Goes to Town," in *Nation's Business*, explained
the widespread success of country music this way: "It
can be explained in just one word: sincerity. When a
hillbilly sings a crazy song, he feels crazy. When he
sings, 'I Laid my Mother Away,' he sees her a-laying
right there in the coffin. He sings more sincere than
most entertainers because the hillbilly was raised
rougher than most entertainers. You got to know a lot

about hard work. You got to have smelt a lot of mule manure before you can sing like a hillbilly. The people who has been raised something like the way the hillbilly has knows what he is singing about and appreciates it."

ORIGINAL CARTER FAMILY

ALVIN PLEASANT CARTER DEC. 15, 1891 — NOV. 7, 1960
SARA CARTER JULY 21, 1899 —
MAYBELLE CARTER MAY 10, 1909 —

A. P. CARTER, HIS WIFE, SARA, AND HIS SISTER-IN-LAW, MAYBELLE, PLAYED IN ONE OF THE FIRST COMMERCIAL COUNTRY RECORDING SESSIONS AT BRISTOL, TENNESSEE. FOR TWO DECADES THEY PERFORMED AS AN UNBEATABLE TEAM. THEIR SONGS BECAME COUNTRY STANDARDS, AND SOME OF A. P.'S ORIGINAL COMPOSITIONS ARE AMONG THE ALL-TIME GREATS. THEY ARE REGARDED BY MANY AS THE EPITOME OF COUNTRY GREATNESS AND ORIGINATORS OF A MUCH COPIED-STYLE.

COUNTRY MUSIC ASSOCIATION

Left, the Carter Family plaque at the Country Music Hall of Fame— *Country Music Assn. photo.* Below, "Miss Country Music," Loretta Lynn— *photo, Decca Records*

11 Country Music Stars and Definitions

In one short chapter, we have room to point out only a few of the giants in the great parade of country music talent.

David Harrison Macon, better known as "Uncle" Dave Macon (also called the "Dixie Dew-Drop," the "king of the banjo pickers," the "king of the hillbillies," and the "Squire of Readyville") was the first top star performer on the Grand Ole Opry. A bundle of energy, flashing a mouthful of gold teeth and a twinkle in his eyes, Uncle Dave charmed audiences with his humor, his enormous collection of rural songs dating back to the 1800's, his singing, and his outstanding skill with the banjo. He joined the Opry in 1925 and was a star performer for fifteen years until shortly before his death. He was in his eighties.

The most influential of all the singing groups in the world of hillbilly music is unquestionably the Carter family. They were Alvin Pleasant ("A. P.") Carter; Sarah Dougherty Carter, his wife; and Maybelle (sometimes spelled "Mae Belle") Addington Carter, A. P.'s sister-in-law. Hailing from the blue ridge mountains of Virginia, this family group sang its close harmony all over the South from 1927 until 1943, during which time they collected, wrote and recorded a tremendous body of authentic country-mountain folk songs. This extensive repertoire of traditional country music has furnished inspiration and material for many of today's folk singers such as Pete Seeger, Joan Baez, the New Lost City Ramblers, Woody Guthrie, Bob Dylan and others as well as modern country-pop singers like Johnny Cash (who incidentally is married to Maybelle Carter's daughter, June). It would be difficult, in fact, to find any performer in the country music field who has not been directly or indirectly influenced by this singing family. The "bluegrass" revival groups are particularly indebted to the pre-commercial music of the Carters.

In their recordings, Sarah sang lead and played chords on the autoharp. A. P. sang bass. Maybelle sang tenor and played guitar. Maybelle played a driving style, using the three bass strings for the melody and fill-in accompaniment on the three treble strings. It put a distinctive flavor in the Carter's music and gives the modern bluegrass musicians a classic form to emulate.

A. P. Carter died in 1960. Sarah, who is retired, lives in California. Maybelle is still active in the country music field, performing with the Johnny Cash troupe.

An album that contains a broad sampling of the Carter family music is RCA Camden's number Cal-2473, titled *Lonesome Pine Special—The Carter Family*. Songs in the album date from their earliest recordings in 1929 to one from their last recording session in 1941. On the album are such traditional classics as "You're Gonna Be Sorry You Let Me Down," "A Distant Land to Roam," "Home in Tennessee," "Darling Little Joe," "Engine One Forty-Three."

Jimmie Rodgers stands as the great single classic figure in modern country western music. His remarkable commercial success pointed the direction country music would take from the early 1930's on. His manner of softer crooning departed from the high-pitched nasal vocals of earlier periods. He was especially known for his famous "blue yodel." The tragic aspects of his life and his early death are the kind of material from which legend springs.

Rodgers was born in Meridian, Mississippi, September 8, 1897. From his early background of railroad work came his image of "the singing brakeman," and his many railroading songs. During most of his life, he knew first hand the hard times and struggle of poor rural people. He was so impoverished at one time, he had to pawn his banjo so he could make it back home to the funeral of his daughter. When he was twenty-seven, a lung hemorrhage put him in the charity ward of a hospital where he nearly died. From then on, he fought a losing struggle with tuberculosis. Not strong enough to continue his railroading job, he turned singer, a thin, tubercular man, struggling over country dirt roads in a second-hand car, his family in tow, making one night stands in jerk-water towns across the South, counting himself lucky if tonight's performance would pay for a cheap hotel room and enough gasoline to make it to the next town. Suddenly, in 1927, when he was twenty-nine years of age, his "losing streak" changed and almost over night he was catapulted into national fame. He made his first record, which brought an initial royalty check of $27.43, but rural audiences were mesmerised by his singing style and before six months had passed, his recording royalties were earning the staggering income of $2,000 a month. He was the first to hit the "rags to riches" country music gold mine trail.

Perhaps country musicians, more than in other fields, are conscious of their success in material terms. That is understandable because so many of them start out poor. The ironic twist to the Jimmie Rodgers story is that during the prosperity boom days of the 1920's, he was starving. Then when the rest of the country was plunged into the darkest days of the depression, at a time when people who had been well off were standing in bread lines and sleeping on park benches, Jimmie Rodgers had traded his second hand car for a new Cadillac and was playing on a $1,500 guitar. From cheap rented rooms, he had moved to a $50,000 mansion—which he called "blue yodler's paradise"—in Kerrville, Texas.

His career lasted only six years. With each passing year, his health grew worse. He was only thirty-five when he made his final trip to the Victor recording studios in New York in his Cadillac with a nurse to help him in his fading hours. He was so weak he had to rest on a cot in the recording studio between numbers. He had completed twelve songs when he suffered a hemorrhage on May 25, 1933, and died early the next morning.

Since that time his records have sold over 20 million copies and he has become one of the world's best known country music singers. His fans stretch from England to Japan. He probably acquired his blues style from country Negro blues singers in Mississippi where he was born, but his recordings also included a wide range, from cowboy and railroad songs to jazz and pop tunes of the day. It was probably his ability to funnel such a wide diversity of music into a distinctive "country" style that headed the music that followed him in the direction of the commercial Nashville country-pop style of today. His plaque in the Country Music Hall of Fame contains the words, "Jimmie Rodgers stands foremost in the country music field as the man who started it all . . . although small in stature, he was a giant among men, starting a trend in the musical taste of millions."

Jimmie Rodgers was mourned by thousands when he died. Many songs of tribute were written and recorded about him. They express more eloquently than any spoken words the feeling country musicians and fans had about him. A collection of these records has been reissued on the RCA album LSP—4073 (e) entitled *When The Evening Shadows Fall,* and includes "The Jimmie Rodgers Blues" (recorded by Elton Britt, Nashville, 1967), "Waiting For a Train" (recorded by Jim Reeves, Meridian, 1956), "The Last Thoughts of Jimmie Rodgers," and "The Passing of Jimmie Rodgers (recorded by Ernest Tubb, San Antonio, 1936), "Jimmie the Kid," and "T.B. Blues" (recorded by Gene Autry, New York, 1931), "When Jimmie Rodgers Said Goodbye" (recorded by Hank Snow, Nashville, 1953), "Jimmie Rodgers' Life," and "The Death of Jimmie Rodgers" (recorded by Bradley Kincaid, New York, 1934), and "We Miss Him When the Evening Shadows Fall" (recorded by Mrs. Jimmie Rodgers, San Antonio, 1936). The album also contains two songs recorded by Jimmie Rodgers, "Whisper Your Mother's Name" and "Yodeling Cowboy," both recorded in Dallas in 1929.

Probably the country-western star to come closest to the Jimmie Rodgers image in recent years, both in his wide appeal to audiences of all kinds and in the legendary aspects of his life and career, was Hank Williams. Williams also was born poor, lived hard, suffered many tragedies, had his brief hour of glory, and died young—even younger than Jimmie Rodgers. He was born in a two-room log cabin in 1923 and died of a heart attack twenty-nine years later, a wealthy and famous man. Between the beginning and end of those twenty-nine years was a life filled with alcohol, drugs, physical suffering from a back injury, and emotional turmoil over a stormy marriage and divorce. After he died in the back seat of one of his five Cadillacs on the way to a performance, twenty-five thousand people attended his funeral. Although he could not read or write a note of music, he composed 125 songs, many of which became country-pop classics. His songs helped nudge country music across the line into commercial pop. Urban pop singers such as Bing Crosby recorded Hank Williams' songs. Among his best known compositions were "Jambalaya," "Cold, Cold Heart," "Hey, Good Lookin'," "You Win Again," and "Your Cheatin' Heart." A Hollywood movie starring George Hamilton which dramatized the life of Hank Williams bore the title of one of his songs, "Your Cheatin' Heart."

Roy Acuff has won the title, "the king of country music." He has been a leader in the field since 1938; composer of such all time classics as "Great Speckled Bird," "Wabash Cannon Ball," and "Wreck on the Highway"; and co-owner of the Acuff-Rose publishing firm, created in 1942, which started the Nashville music publishing industry. Acuff is in the Country Music Hall of Fame, as is Ernest Tubb, known as the "Texas Troubadour," and Tex Ritter, also a Texan.

Hank Snow, a Nova Scotia farm boy who was heavily influenced by Jimmie Rodgers, called himself the "Yodeling Ranger." Snow and Ernest Tubb closely associated their careers with the legend of Jimmie Rodgers. In fact, Rodgers' widow passed Jimmie Rodgers' guitar on to Ernest Tubb because of the similarity of their styles.

Eddie Arnold, the "Tennessee Plowboy," began his snowballing success in the 1940's. The Victor recording company had, by 1947, sold nearly three million Eddie Arnold records. His recording of "That's How Much I Love You" and "Don't Rob Another Man's Castle" were some of his biggest hits. His singing style, pleasing and smooth, typifies the modern approach to country western songs.

Jim Reeves, another East Texas country boy, enjoyed a great country-pop success in the late fifties and early sixties, until he died in an airplane crash in 1964. Like Eddie Arnold, his singing style was popular with urban as well as country listeners, and he could transcend the "country music" category while still maintaining the country music identity.

This brings us to some of today's big names such as Porter Wagoner, Don Gibson, George Hamilton IV, Johnny Cash, Glen Campbell, Roger Miller and Chet Atkins, to list but a few.

Don Gibson shows the blues "soul" and rock influence in his style, which is emotionally very appealing. A composer as well as a guitarist and singer, he has written such classics as "I Can't Stop Loving You" and "Oh, Lonesome Me."

Gibson's style underscores how far rural music has moved toward up-town sophistication. George Hamilton IV draws a fine line between country-pop and its cousin, urban folk-pop. Chet Atkins towers above all the instrumentalists as Mr. Nashville of the 1970's. In fact, he has been credited with creating the

Nashville sound (however you may care to define that elusive element). He is a fine guitarist. Unlike guitar players in the 1930 Western swing bands who played a kind of rustic jazz improvisation that was scorned by real jazz musicians, Atkins commands the respect of all musicians whether he is playing jazz, pop, or country style. He again exemplifies the modern Nashville recording artist who has brought a high degree of musicianship to country music while still able to keep its flavor. Admirers of Chet Atkins say it was he who made country music respectable. He is the chief of RCA Victor's Country Music division.

Another competent musician who has scored high in the country-pop area is tenor saxophonist Boots Randolph. His "yackety sax" style has been widely imitated, but while he uses the ricky-tick approach for country flavor, he is a capable jazz performer as well.

Roger Miller has gained for himself a unique niche among country-pop composers. He has been a leader in the trend toward clever, amusing novelty songs. Not only his compositions, but his relaxed, off-beat personality have made a big impact on the entire world of show business, from the record industry to television. His presence before an audience is a striking example of how country-pop entertainers have moved from the rustic, hayseed stereotype to the smooth, urban "swinger." Departing from the "weepers," his songs are witty, often nonsensical novelty songs such as, "Dang Me," "You Can't Roller-Skate in a Buffalo Herd," "I Loved My Uncle Till She Died," and his most famous "King of the Road."

One of the "hottest" names on the Nashville scene is Johnny Cash. His last name couldn't be more appropriate, for his success as a singer, TV personality and movie star has earned vast amounts. By now it is becoming a cliché to point out the early poverty and hardships of these country stars, but how else can one give the facts of this brooding, intense balladeer? He was born in a shack in Arkansas in 1932 during the darkest days of the depression and nearly died of malnutrition as a child. He was working as a not very successful door-to-door salesman when he got his first recording contract in 1955. Soon after, he joined the "Louisiana Hayride" show and then in 1956 recorded the outstanding hit "I Walk the Line." From then on, he had it made as a singer and composer.

Although country music has drawn heavily on Negro culture for its blues and guitar styling, there have been few black entertainers in the realm of hillbilly music. The tradition of segregation practiced in the South has been described by some writers as the reason for the absence of Negro hillbilly musicians, however that is a curious anomaly since other types of popular music had their birthplace in the South and were heavily represented by black musicians: jazz in New Orleans, ragtime in Joplin, Missouri, the blues all over. Either the rural sections where country music flourished were more rigidly segregated, or—a possibility that is overlooked by students of the field—it is quite likely also that country music, especially the Appalachian mountain styles where few Negroes lived, did not appeal to black performers as a form of expression with which they felt comfortable. A noteable exception to all of this is Charley Pride who is a highly popular and successful country-western singer and recording star.

Women's liberation came late to the country music field. Until World War II, it was pretty much a man's domain; perhaps that was why more songs were written about woman's fickle nature than man's shortcomings. Again, the cultural traditions of the rural South which gave a clear definition to a woman's role as mother and homemaker came into play here. Even though a number of women are today becoming top-selling Nashville stars, the old values linger on. When Tennessee's former governor Frank Clement was praising the success of country singer Kitty Wells, he was quick to add that she was at the same time, "an outstanding wife and mother, in keeping with the traditions of Southern womanhood."

It was in the 1940's that the ladies began having their say. Rosalie Allen, Jenny Lou Carson and Molly O'Day were among the first girl singers to make the popularity charts and they were followed by Kitty Wells and Rose Maddox.

Kitty Wells' success dates from 1952 when she recorded "It Wasn't God Who Made Honky Tonk Angels." She has been called the "queen of country music." Some of her recordings in the ever-popular "weeper" category include "I Gave My Wedding Dress Away" and "Heartbreak U.S.A."

Many of the fair sex are as successful at composing songs as singing them. Jenny Lou Carson can list among her hit compositions the "standard" country classic, "Jealous Heart."

Today's list of top female Nashville recording artists would also include Loretta Lynn, Melba Montgomery, Skeeter Davis, Dottie West, Norma Jean, Jean Shepard, Tammy Wynette, Marion Worth, Jeannie Seely, Wanda Jackson, Jan Howard and Connie Smith.

The ladies have added a whole new dimension—

and a delightful one—to country singing. From a musical standpoint, many are quite talented. Besides, we now have the woman's viewpoint. For example, in one of her albums, Loretta Lynn warns her man "Don't Come Home A-Drinkin' (With Lovin' on Your Mind)." She also demands, "What Kind of Girl Do You Think I Am?" As for the problem of the eternal triangle, Loretta Lynn sings confidently, "You Ain't Woman Enough (To Get My Man)."

One gal who came to Nashville and really hit the big time is Tammy Wynette. She became the first of the female country singers to have an album sell in excess of a million dollars. For the past four years (at the time of this writing), she has won the Country Music Association of America's top female vocalist award plus two Grammies as best female vocalist. The emotional despair and sob in her voice have placed her in the unique position of being a 'soul' singer—country style. Her audience is international. Beatle Ringo Starr once asked to watch a Tammy Wynette recording date in Nashville, which would seem to indicate the popular music gulf between London rock and Nashville country is not so wide as one might think.

Tammy rejects the women's liberation movement with her recording "Don't Liberate Me (Love Me)." She lauds her feminine role with "The Joy of Being a Woman" but also warns "Your Good Girl's Gonna Go Bad." However, on other recordings she takes the role of the loyal sweetheart, "Make Me Your Kind of Woman" and "My Arms Stay Open Late." She has composed or co-written many of her own hits, inculding 1969 Grammy award winner in which she gives this advice to other women, "Stand By Your Man."

The addition of female vocalists has been one of

the many improvements that have come to modern country music. It is another in the changes that is making this a kind of popular music that will no doubt appeal to a wider and wider audience in the years ahead.

Some Definitions

Event song. A category of country songs in which the subject matter of the lyrics deals with a specific event such as a mine disaster, train wreck, presidential election, death of a prominent figure, etc. Some examples are: "Cowards over Pearl Harbor," "The Death of Floyd Collins," "The Death of Hank Williams," "Franklin Roosevelt's Back Again," "The John T. Scopes Trial."

Bluegrass. One of the styles of country music, associated with the mountain music of North Carolina, Tennessee, Kentucky and Virginia. It is traditional in nature, using no amplified guitars and no drums, and generally relying on the five-string banjo, string bass, mandolin, guitar and fiddle, plus occasionally the harmonica and accordian. There is a movement known as the "bluegrass revival" which rejects the commercial pop sound of Nashville for the more old-time string band sound. Some of these groups are the Stanley Brothers, the Country Gentlemen and Flatt and Scruggs. The term *bluegrass* is said to be derived from the Blue Grass Boys, the name of Bill Monroe's string band which was formed in 1938. Monroe has been called the "father of bluegrass music."

Rockabilly. The stronger rhythmic "rock" tempos have influenced many country singers and musicians. In some cases, they have combined country songs with a rock beat, and the resulting combination has been called *rockabilly.* The Everly Brothers are an example. But the impact of rock-and-roll can be heard in the styles of singers such as Johnny Cash, Don Gibson and many others. A semi-rock-and-roll background has given any number of country songs a popularity nudge in the direction of the younger audiences.

The Nashville Sound is one of those elusive musical nuances that are difficult to define in exact terms, music being an art rather than a science. Chet Atkins and the Owen Bradley recording studios are often mentioned as pioneers in this area. Basically, it is a large sound that depends to a great extent on the skill of the recording engineers, who handle their mixing boards and echo chambers with the finesse of virtuosos. The recording engineer virtually becomes part of the musical group by the manner in which he doctors tapes to produce an over all saleable product. Choral backgrounds are generally used, with electric guitar the predominating instrument. Such terms as "relaxed," "loose," "easygoing beat" have been employed to describe the sound. By the devices of dubbing and recording sound-with-sound, a singer might come out voicing several harmony parts with himself, or herself. (This, however, was not invented in Nashville. Les Paul and Mary Ford did it with great success in the early 1950's.)

Above, Woody Guthrie—*RCA Records photo.* Below, Joan Baez—*photo, courtesy Warner Brothers, Inc., and George Nichols*

12 Folk Singing—Country Music's City Cousin

Country music is primarily the music of white America, especially the blue collar worker. It deals with personal and spiritual matters rather than with social problems. Folk singing, which had much the same roots as country music, branched off in the 1930's to concern itself more with class struggles and political ideology. It found an audience in the urban intellectual circles and has become these days the protest voice of the young. Matters ranging from civil rights to welfare, the Viet Nam war and pollution have been voiced by folk singers. In the 1960's, it felt, as did most branches of music, the influence of the rock beat. Many folk singers adopted the folk-rock style.

When the subject of folk singing comes up, three names immediately spring to mind, Woody Guthrie, Burl Ives, and Bob Dylan. Guthrie, because his dust bowl songs of social injustice in the 1930's and his legendary life style set the direction the urban folk movement would take; Burl Ives, because he popularized folk singing to a large audience; and Bob Dylan, because he especially caught the young people's imagination in the 1960's and 1970's, and became their poet and spokesman.

There are other names of equal importance in
their own right, of course: Joan Baez, Pete Seeger,
Tom Paxton, Phil Ochs, Josh White, and groups such
as Peter, Paul and Mary, and The Weavers.

Woodrow Wilson Guthrie, known to his many
fans as Woody, was born in Okemah, Oklahoma, July
14, 1912, and grew up amidst the boom and bust days
of the Southwest's oil fields and depression. By the
time he was fifteen, he was on his own, finding jobs
where he could and eventually trekking along with
the impoverished dust bowl Oakies out to California
in the 1930's, like a character right out of the pages of
Grapes of Wrath. Woody knew first hand the despair
and struggle of the Oakies. The experiences he had
among the rural poor gave him material for a lifetime
of writing, and a prolific writer he was. During a relatively brief career, he produced a thousand songs,
hundreds of stories and articles and three books. Some
of his best known songs are "This Land Is Your Land,"
"So Long It's Been Good to Know You," "Oklahoma
Hills," "Tom Joad," "Hard Travelin'," "The Philadelphia Lawyer," and "The Big Grand Coulee Dam."

When Guthrie dust-bowled it out to California in
the 1930's, he was just another scrawny country
singer carrying a beat-up guitar, and he got a job singing hillbilly on a Los Angeles radio station. The tunes
he sang he had picked up in his meanderings around
Texas and Oklahoma and from Carter Family recordings.

But Woody had a great sense of social awareness,
and the sights he'd seen of people going hungry, often
treated as sub-human, got under his skin. He began
writing songs to express his anger about how the

Oakies had been thrown out of their homes and land and left penniless refugees on the side of the road. This was his metamorphosis from a hillbilly guitar picker to a front-line protest folk singer. Songs he wrote about the troubles of the Oakies include "Dust Bowl Refugee," "Talking Dust Bowl Blues," and "I Ain't Got No Home in This World Anymore." He called for "socialized medicine, socialized living, socialized working, socialized thinking, socialized resting, socialized sleeping, socialized seeding, and socialized breeding."

In 1938, he packed up his guitar and suitcase full of songs and hied himself to New York where he recorded his *Dust Bowl Ballads* for RCA Victor. These records, along with radio broadcasts, made him a folk hero in urban intellectual circles. The liberals heard in his songs the cries of the oppressed against a system they wanted to change. From that time on, Woody Guthrie dropped his hillbilly image and became a folk protest singer par excellance. His life-style of the wandering poet and balladeer, guitar slung on his back, his rejection of The Establishment, created an image that aspiring young folk singers who followed him tried to emulate. By his own self-description, he was "a ramblin' man, a hobo."

We keep coming back to the Carter Family in our examination of country and folk singing. Many of Woody's songs were based on folk melodies recorded by the Carter family. Their "Wildwood Flower" became Guthrie's World War II song, "The Reuben James." His well known patriotic song, "This Land," was a combination of the melodies from the Carter's "When the World's on Fire," and "Little Darling Pal

of Mine." Many other lyrics Guthrie composed were
set to Carter family melodies. Since these traditional
mountain ballads go back many years, in some cases
as much as two hundred and more, the original composer has long been forgotten and the melody is in the
public domain; that is to say, the tune is no longer
protected by copyright and anyone is free to use it. It
is a common practice for folk singers to use the old
traditional melodies as vehicles for their poetry. This
sometimes happens in other branches of the pop field.
The Elvis Presley ballad hit of the 1950's, "Love Me
Tender," for example, was originally the melody of a
traditional song called "Aura Lee."

While Guthrie's songs protested social injustice,
many also were intensely patriotic compositions. Such
a song is "This Land Is Your Land," probably his best
known work.

In 1950, he entered a Brooklyn, New York, hos-
pital, stricken with an incurable nerve disease called
Huntington's Chorea, which had been his mother's
fatal illness. After being hospitalized for 17 years,
Woody died in 1967. His son, Arlo, is now the Guthrie
folk singer known to the current young generation.
Arlo is gaining recognition since his movie, *Alice's
Restaurant*.

Back in the "tail end section" of Woody's birthplace, Okemah, in eastern Oklahoma, is his childhood
home. A two-story house built of orange-brown sand-
stone and lumber, Woody called it the "old London
House," after the family who had previously owned it.
There are no signs directing the tourist to the home or
any kind of monument, statue, or formal sign indi-
cating this is Woody Guthrie's home town. On a wall

of the weather-beaten old house where he lived are scrawled in red the words, "Here once lived one of the greatest Americans the world has ever known and his name was Woody." This and the memories of people who knew him and his songs are about the only monuments we have of a man many consider to be America's greatest folk singer.

On the anniversary of Woody's birthday in 1971, his widow, Marjorie, and their son, Arlo, presented a collection of his records and books to the town library. The Okemah Chamber of Commerce, however, decided against an official Woody Guthrie Day celebration. Residents feared too much of an invasion of hippies. Woody probably would have loved the kids, especially if they brought their guitars.

In the early 1950's, Burl Ives became known on a wider scale with the general public than Woody Guthrie. Ives sang a great variety of American folk songs— not principally of the protest category—in an appealing, engaging manner. His mellow voice and striking appearance put his singing on a nationwide pop basis. Soon, thousands of amateur folk enthusiasts were buying Burl Ives song books and taking guitar lessons. Hootnannies became the rage and folk festivals became annual events. One popular center of hootnanny activities during the 1950's and 1960's was Washington Square in Greenwich Village. At the Metropole, a little bar near Times Square, there was a regular Sunday afternoon jam session where one could hear such famous jazz musicians as Coleman Hawkins, Roy Eldridge, Marty Napoleon, Henry "Red" Allen, to name only a few. From there, if the weather was pleasant, one could travel down to Washington

Square and listen to the folk musicians who gathered
in the park. Each had his individual audience clus-
tered around him, listening. Some were lone singers,
accompanying themselves with their guitars. Others
were string bands, using the colorful homemade bass
improvised from a wash tub, broomstick and rope. In
March, 1961, the New York City Commissioner of
Parks banned folk singing in Washington Square. The
folk singers got up in arms, protested, nearly rioted,
took the matter to court and by July the Appellate
Division of the Supreme Court ruled against the Park
Commissioner, and the folk singers were back doing
their thing in the park.

When Woody Guthrie was forced by failing
health to lay down his guitar, a scrawny youngster
just out of his teens was moving into the scene to pick
it up. His name is Robert Zimmerman, better known
the world over by the name he adopted, Bob Dylan.

Dylan is an enigmatic young man who keeps to
himself a good deal of the time and has generated an
air of mystique about his goings and his comings, not
to mention his writings. Critics can't seem to agree on
exactly what he is saying, but young people say they
trust what he is telling them. His popularity with the
under-thirty generation is unquestioned.

What he has accomplished, he has done in a
hurry. To give an illustration of his meteoric rise to
world fame, a book I was recently perusing on the subject of folk singers, published in 1962, did not even
mention Dylan. Today, anything being written about
the world of pop music must list Dylan among the
front ranks of the folk-rock innovators. He arrived in
New York in 1961 when he was twenty. By the time he

was twenty-five he was a world-wide legend. He then retired and went into seclusion following a serious motorcycle accident, reappeared on the music scene two years later and wound up his thirtieth year a millionaire several times over. During these ten years, he has kept music critics in a constant state of turmoil over his creative mutations. First he was a writer of fiery protest songs. Then he shook everybody up by appearing with an amplified guitar and putting a rock beat to his folk singing. No sooner was the pop music world settling down from that shock when he racked up his bike and vanished from the public eye, thus loosing a flood of rumors about whether he would ever perform again. Perform again he did, but when he reappeared, his songs were more detached from political matters, in some ways as surrealistic as ever, but in a different vein. His more recent albums have some critics glumly reporting that he has gotten rich, soft and commercial, while others mention Zen, transcendentalism, mysticism and suggest that Dylan is trying to tell us something about the ultimate reality and experiencing God.

This young man—whatever critics say about him —has evidently single-handedly given a new dimension to American pop music, making it the literature of the rock age. He has sold 10 million albums in the United States and generated a fierce loyalty among his following.

One of his ardent fans, a young man named Alan J. (A. J.) Weberman, has busied himself at the full-time pursuit of establishing a Dylan archive. His collection contains virtually everything Dylan has written or said, as well as a multitude of Dylan souvenirs and trivia, some of them collected by poking through the garbage from Dylan's Greenwich Village apartment. Weberman's obsessive preoccupation with Bob Dylan's career dates back to 1965 when Dylan switched to his folk rock style. Had Dylan gone off on a fantasy nonsense kick, or was he really saying something, Weberman wanted to know. A. J. came to the conclusion that Dylan was making some profound pronouncements through his songs, but it would require an "analytical method of criticism" to understand the metaphors and symbols. Weberman then set out on the ambitious task of compiling a concordance which consists of two thick volumes of computer printouts that have every word written by Dylan in alphabetical order cross-indexed to the original lines in which it appeared. He claims only through such careful and scholarly approach can one understand the poetic universe in which Dylan's creative thoughts exist. Whether all this is fan-worship carried to the final extreme, or a useful scholarly accomplishment, it has made Weberman something of a celebrity in the folk-rock subculture and someone to be reckoned with in matters of "Dylanology" as he terms it. And in either case, it illustrates how firmly the Dylan legend is already established in the folk-rock world.

This poet of the folk-rock space age, Robert Zimmerman, was born in Duluth, Minnesota, in 1941. He taught himself to play guitar and harmonica and organized a rock'n'roll band in high school. Once out of school, he changed his name to Dylan, went through the drifting stage that many folk singers experience. He visited Woody Guthrie in a New Jersey hospital in 1960 and is said to have become close friends with the dying folk singer. Perhaps some of Woody's speech patterns rubbed off because from then on, Dylan had a bit of a Southwestern, twangy drawl not exactly in character with his Minnesota background. He appeared in New York, singing in Greenwich Village coffee houses in 1961, a skinny kid with a great shock of hair and a thin, intense face. That was his hot protest period. His success with the young can be dated from his early composition, "The Times They Are A-Changin' " which clearly drew the battle lines of the youth rebellion. It was an outspoken song of revolution, telling the mothers and fathers (the older generation) in no uncertain terms that their ways were dated, that their sons and daughters were beyond their command, and to stop criticizing what they couldn't understand. Naturally most kids dug the song and Dylan became their leader and spokesman. In 1962, at the climax of the Newport Folk Festival, singers like Joan Baez and Pete Seeger joined Dylan to sing his "Blowin' in the Wind," a cry against racial oppression which became closely associated with the civil rights movement of the 1960's.

With mounting success and fame came a hectic pace as Dylan raced around the country from concert dates to recording studios. It was a period during which he resorted to drugs to prop up his tired body, a practice he has since strongly rejected.

It was at the 1965 Newport Festival that he introduced the amplified guitar as a new rhythmic rock instrument to accompany folk singing. The audience was at first appalled and booed him off the stage, but young rock fans thought the idea was groovy and soon his new sound was influencing top rock stars like Simon and Garfunkle and the Beatles.

Bob Dylan's musical career falls roughly into

three divisions. First were the early years in which he accompanied his own singing, a time when his poetry of protest was its most outspoken. "Blowin' in the Wind," "The Times They Are A-Changin'," "Masters of the War," and "Who Killed Davey Moore?" were written during that period. The second division, characterized by an amplified guitar rock rhythm, produced the big hit, "Mr. Tambourine Man." The third stage in his career came after he recovered from his accident and resulted in albums such as *John Wesley Harding, Nashville Skyline, Self-Portrait,* and *New Morning.* These have a smoother commercial sound with a country-western background. Dylan seems to have gone the full circle of folk music back to its country-western roots.

It would be difficult to decipher Dylan's charisma. As the song goes, "When You're Hot, You're Hot." And Dylan hit hot with his public in the folk-rock field. His ability as a performer might be open to question. He wouldn't win any prizes with his wheezy harmonica playing, his ability with the guitar is only average and his singing would drive anyone with any degree of musical sensitivity right up the wall. His achievements lie in the area of composer and poet. Certainly he has written highly successful pop tunes. They are current with top performing groups from Peter, Paul and Mary to Lawrence Welk. His early protest lyrics made clear-cut timely statements that smoked like a hot branding iron sizzling on tender hide. Then his poetry took on an enigmatic, rambling context. He has been called a mystic perhaps because of the elusive meaning of his lyrics. That might be an asset; everyone is free to make his own interpretation.

In his songs, Dylan often employs the devices of repetition, symbolism and a kind of free-association, stream-of-consciousness poetry. Either he is getting around to saying some very profound things or he has run out of anything to say and is just putting everyone on. It will be interesting to see how his career will develop from this point.

A good introduction to Dylan is Columbia's album KCS 9463, *Bob Dylan's Greatest Hits*, which contains samplings from many of his top albums. Also, thrown in for *pelón*, is a large, psychedelic poster of Dylan. Who can pass up a bargain like that?

Many people who have heard and enjoyed Dylan's songs never heard Dylan sing them, and might not have enjoyed them nearly so much if they had. It was the polished vocal group of Peter Yarrow, Paul Stookey, and Mary Travers, better known as Peter, Paul and Mary (or "Two Beards and a Blonde") who popularized many of Dylan's songs. Their smooth, close harmony and sophisticated treatment took the twangy, primitive sound of the Guthries and the Dylans and gave folk-singing a palatability acceptable to a wide audience. As a result the trio became highly successful in the 1960's, especially with the college age audience. Some of their hit recordings were "500 Miles," "This Train," "Cruel War," "If I Had a Hammer," and "Where Have All The Flowers Gone?"

The old cliché, "There is nothing new in the world," can be applied to contemporary protest folk singing. Indeed, as far back as the 11th century, in southern France, northern Italy, and northern Spain, there existed a famous class of poet-musicians known as troubadours who wrote about the politics of their

day. The era of the troubadours lasted until the 13th
century, and during this period, these singers had a
great freedom of speech for their time. Their poetry,
often satirical, had a strong social influence on the
times. The wandering adventurers of that bygone era
who expressed their political convictions in song
would no doubt find a kinship with today's folk-rock
protest people.

   If I were to make any criticism of the folk-protest
movement, it would be directed at its lack of humor.
The protest songs of the 1960's were often biting and
bitterly honest. But they were short on humor of the
satirical variety. Satire, according to Webster, is a
form of trenchant wit, irony or sarcasm. It can be the
most vitriolic form of criticism, yet the element of humor, black though it might be, is still present. One
protest folk-singer who not only did not neglect satire,
but made it his chief stock-in-trade, was Tom Lehrer,
a college mathematics professor turned song writer
and performer. During the late 1950's and early
1960's, he produced a number of satirical protest-type
albums that poked fun at the foibles and shortcomings of our society. Nothing escaped his acid wit. He
even wrote a protest folk song making fun of protest
folk singing. He enjoyed considerable popularity
among audiences of college age levels and up, but
didn't catch on with the younger crowd. There were
several strikes against him in that area; being a college professor he was automatically a member of The
Establishment. Too, he committed the sin of playing
that extinct instrument, the piano, instead of a guitar,
and compounded the felony by using a kind of ragtime style instead of rock. But his biggest transgres-

sion was in not taking himself seriously enough and in putting down the pervading vogue of significance and relevance seeking. His songs should not be misconstrued as representing his true convictions, he said, for he had none. "If anyone objects to any statement I make," he said, "I am quite prepared not only to retract it, but also to deny under oath that I ever made it!"

Protest folk singing expresses very strongly the views of one area of our society. From the 1930's to the 1970's, it has been the voice of the left-wing, anti-war, pro-civil rights, anti-establishment people. But as the title of Bob Dylan's song said, "The Times They Are A-Changing." He was speaking of another time and another decade now past, but the title can be re-applied to a new time, a new change now upon us. In our opening chapter we observed that popular music is in a constant state of flux. This is as true of folk singing as of Tin Pan Alley or country-western. Perhaps even more so, because folk singers are the avant-guarde, in the front lines struggling with the newest problems of our land. At one time the problems of the dust bowl Oakies were urgent and timely. Now songs about that era have become historical pieces from a remote past. In the 1960's, civil rights, the Viet Nam war, President Lyndon Johnson, and The Establishment were hot issues with folk singers. Folk singing provided the symbols and the heroes of the militant young demonstrators in the 1960's and had a real part in directing the events of the decade. Then the war began winding down. Many of the civil rights battles had been won. The trend toward socialism which folk singers had so long championed was becoming a more evident reality. But a socialized, homogenized society has its own problems, namely a loss of individual identity, a surrender of privacy. These are matters the young people of the 1970's are sensing and beginning to write poetry about. And they are aware of our industrialization that has brought material benefits but a loss of life quality. Especially are they aware of the threat to ecology—to the very existence of human life on this planet—by pollution and over-population. These are important issues to inspire songs of concern and protest.

Facing such staggering, seemingly insurmountable problems, the young people, in their need for some cosmic foundation, appear to be searching for the old gods that previous generations have let die. On campuses across the nation, there is a reaching for the spiritual. From the Maharishi's Eastern transcendentalism to *Jesus Christ, Superstar,* the search goes on for something man needs perhaps even more than a society where everyone has a guaranteed income and a color television set. Every few generations, mankind rediscovers a basic fact about himself, namely that he has a spiritual side to his nature restlessly seeking a final cosmic reality to this frightening dream we call life. This may be the new direction folk-rock will take in an effort to comprehend and express in poetry and music what analytical language and science cannot.

Elvis Presley—*RCA Records photo*

13　The Revolution in Popular Music

In the 1950's, a revolution began in America. There was nothing quiet about it, yet, like many revolutions, it had already happened before most people woke up to what was going on. It has been one of the most curious social revolutions in our history. Never before have the young people banded together, splintered off into a compartment totally their own, where they formed their own culture, economy and morals. And never before has a generation of young people been so totally immersed in its own music—so much that the music itself symbolized, reflected, often dictated the very nature of its revolution. The "Lost Generation" of the 1920's had its hot jazz, but their music was a part of the Saturday night dances, the fraternity parties, the speakeasies, the wind-up Victrolas. They didn't live with it the greater part of every day. On the other hand, they didn't have the equipment we have now. With compact tape recorders and transistor radios, a youngster these days can walk around with a whole rock band in his pocket—and usually does.

To say, "It all began with Elvis" has become as much of a cliché as "Jazz began in New Orleans and went up the river to Chicago."

Well, clichés often become what they are because they simply repeat unalterable facts. And Elvis *was* the big turning point. But in this case, I think we tend to overlook some trends in the early 1950's which give us clues that America was growing tired of its pop music styles. Among the crooners, relaxation was the mode in vogue. Perry Como all but dozed while he was singing. It was cool, and very good. But then, in the early 1950's, along came a frail young man wearing an enormous hearing aid who sweated and sobbed and got down on his knees and bared his soul to his audience. And he was a sensation. Johnnie Ray. He was a pioneer, one of the first of a new breed of pop singers who would pour raw, uninhibited emotion into their singing. Sure it was commercial, but America grabbed it. We bought his recording of "Cry" as if tomorrow depended on it.

At the same time, in the black culture, rhythm and blues singers were doing it in an even gutsier way, though not much of their music was seeping out into the white audiences.

Then, upon the restrained, enervated pop music scene, like a nuclear explosion, burst rock'n'roll.

Two factors appear to have contributed to the success of the rock movement. One was economic; the other had to do with the direction jazz had been taking since the 1940's.

John Philip Sousa, "the March King," is said to have once remarked that jazz music would endure as long as people heard it through their feet and not their heads. Until the end of World War II, America's youth had been hearing jazz through their feet. It had been music to dance to, music to move to. It had a beat— Lord, did it ever! But then jazz musicians became cerebral. They began experimenting with involved scales and way-out harmonies. A music form needs to change and develop or it becomes stagnant, but jazz performers became so involved with complicated new ideas that they forgot about the beat. "Cool" became the order of the day. It was hip for jazz soloists to turn their back on the crowd, ignore it, and often walk off the stand in the middle of a tune to express their disdain for the chumps who had paid five bucks to come hear them. Jazz was no longer fun and healthy, something to make you laugh and clap your hands. Some of the new, progressive styles—bop and "cool"—had become neurotic, ingrown.

Jazz became so complicated and mathematical that one almost had to have a degree in music to understand what was going on. Jazz followers became an increasingly small, intense, esoteric group. And what had become of the beat, that great pulse that began throbbing way back in the New Orleans honky-tonks and had kept jazz alive and rosy-cheeked all those years? It was "implied" rather than "stated" said the new genre of avant-guarde jazzmen. They didn't want to be confined by a strong two or four-beat measure. In some styles, the bass drum no longer supplied a steady beat; it was used to accent the solos with intermittent explosions while the cymbals weakly maintained the beat. The kids, who were sitting around trying to look intellectual while some cat on a bandstand was running scales and finger exercises on his instrument and calling it a jazz solo, were not getting much soul satisfaction out of a beat that was implied. They were hungry for the real thing.

Kids are crammed with energy. Muscles are screaming for action. Glands are pouring sex hormones through young blood. They are *alive*, and they need to express it, all the way back to that primitive ritual of dancing around a campfire to the pounding beat on a hollow log. How are you going to do that to a kind of music where the beat is only implied?

Before World War I, America had been a less crowded country. Young people, for the most part, had lived in small towns or in the country. There were plenty of room and enough activities to dispell the excess energy. One could ride a horse, swim in the creek, chop wood, or just run in any direction and yell at the top of one's lungs. Then the world began crowding in. A young person's life became increasingly confined and restricted. In the 1920's, dancing the Charleston to hot jazz was an outlet. Then big band swing came along with a solid four-to-the-measure beat, and with it, the jitterbug. But following World War II, big bands faded out and there wasn't much to really get excited about. The pop music scene wasn't much help. Male singers like Eddie Fisher, Harry Belafonte, Mario Lanza and Tony Bennett were good, but they were grown-up and smooth and polished. So were girl vocalists like Lena Horne, Julie London and Rosemary Clooney.

While jazz and urban pop were committing suicide, there was a native American music that had not only not forgotten the beat; it had juiced it up with twentieth century electronics. It was blues in the Negro community—the delta blues gone electrified and vital. Rhythm'n'blues. But it was heard only in the black communities. Somebody had to introduce it to the white kids.

The stage was set. Out of the wings stepped a young Memphis truck driver with a ducktail hair style and a sullen, brooding expression; Elvis Presley with his rock'n'roll guitar. He was by no means first. In 1954, a Negro group, the Chords, had played the rock-

'n'roll style—rhythm'n'blues combined with country-western—and in 1955, Bill Haley and a white group, the Comets, recorded the hit "Rock Around the Clock." But they lacked Elvis's charisma. More to the point, they lacked his sex appeal. When Elvis came on, he did more than sing. He went through a whole series of gyrations filled with sexual implications. It was crude, it was vulgar, it was primitive—and just the thing for the mood of the hour. His voice trembled and cried out. His guitar thundered. His torso did bumps and grinds and shimmies. And a whole generation of young people blew its cool.

A New York disk jockey, Alan Freed, put a name to it: "Rock'n'roll." He got the idea from a raunchy old blues number, "My baby rocks me with a steady roll." (Like jazz, rock'n'roll got its name from a slang expression with sexual implications, a derivation that has generally been forgotten.)

The adult population hit the ceiling. Almost everyone out of his teens unanimously condemned the new music. It would be the downfall of American youth. Elvis was considered a prophet of Satan. (In private life, he was actually a polite young man who said "Sir" and "Ma'am" to his elders, recited his prayers every night, and was disturbed by his unexpected success.)

Elvis's career began when he appeared on a country music stage show in Memphis. He was then an unknown 19-year-old. Sam Phillips, who was the head of a Memphis record company called Sun Records heard about him and got him to record, using the Negro rhythm'n'blues style. The upshot of all that was the sale of Presley's recording contract to RCA Victor records for $40,000. Elvis then appeared on the Jimmy

Dorsey TV show and subsequently on the Ed Sullivan show (but only after Sullivan instructed his cameramen to show the young singer only from the belt buckle up). That was 1956. By 1960, Elvis had sold $120 million worth of records, sheet music and movie tickets, and he'd gone from driving a truck to owning a fleet of Cadillacs.

Earlier, we mentioned the economic factor in rock'n'roll's success. With all the fulminating grown-ups were doing about the new rock sounds, they had themselves to blame, though few realized it. Adults simply were not buying enough records. It was the teenagers who had become the record buying consumers of America. The post-war baby boom was growing into the teenage population, and they had plenty of money to spend. By 1958, 70 percent of all records sold were going to teenagers. Obviously, the recording companies, wanting to stay in business, cut down on their production of adult pop and jazz records and concentrated on what the teenagers were demanding —rock'n'roll.

Radio stations, their network entertainment shows gobbled up by television, were turning to recorded music programming. The sales of records were mounting in huge leaps. It was a rare teenager who didn't own a record player and/or a radio, and most of the time it was playing the new rock music.

Out of this has grown a rock music oriented culture. People in their early thirties today—young business executives, professional people and housewives —grew up on rock. To many of them it is the only kind of pop music they are comfortable with.

Some maintain that rock music was a symptom

of increasing sociological disturbances and moral up-
heavals in American life. Certainly there were many
developments to back their views. Following World
War II, all our old Puritan attitudes began toppling.
We became increasingly preoccupied with sex while
at the same time crime and violence were on the increase.

Publishing trends reflected the changing times.
America bought 27 million copies of Mickey Spillane's
Mike Hammer books that dripped sadism and sex.
Peyton Place, a novel based on small town sin, be-
came one of the biggest best sellers of all times. Dr.
Alfred C. Kinsey went around asking very personal
questions and published the answers in his 1948 best
seller, *Sexual Behavior in the Human Male*. Playboy
Magazine appeared on the newsstand with center
fold-out nudes.

Meanwhile, teenagers were rising to a head-on
confrontation with adult authority. There appeared on
the scene a young movie actor who personified the re-
bellious attitude of the troubled adolescent. He was
James Dean. He summed up the image in his most
famous motion picture, *Rebel Without a Cause*. Then
he got killed in his speeding car at dusk and cinched
his immortality. Teenagers all over the world had a
dead hero, a legend, a symbol.

By the mid-1950's, the teenage mass challenge
of adult authority was spreading like wildfire. In New
York in 1956, teenage murderers had increased 26 percent over the year before. The 36 percent increase in
auto thefts and 92 percent rise in possession of dangerous weapons was attributed to teenagers. "Juvenile
delinquency" became the phrase of the hour.

Movies spelled out this new breed and their tough, violent flaunting of authority. *The Wild Ones* portrayed Marlon Brando as the leader of a leather-jacketed motorcycle gang that rode into a small town, took it over and terrorized the citizens. Evan Hunter wrote *Blackboard Jungle,* a novel dramatizing the violence and loss of control in public schools.

No matter how polite Elvis might have been in private, his public image exuded that sullen, defiant attitude that teenagers espoused.

Viewed from this angle, rock'n'roll music with its crude, primitive sound, explosive excitement, sexual implications and over-all sneer at the adult world certainly does appear to fit the times in which it was born. And in the decade that followed, the 1960's, one can hardly visualize the drug and sex scene without the accompaniment of acid rock or the hippie culture without the big beat.

A wave of riots followed the first rock concerts in 1956. At Newport, R.I., the U.S. Navy banned the playing of rock'n'roll music at the enlisted men's club because of a chair-smashing, bottle-throwing riot that culminated a rock'n'roll session.

The same thing was happening in other parts of the world. Police had to quell riots in Oslo, Norway; Melbourne, Australia; Singapore, Malaysia; and London, England. Over a hundred youths were arrested in England during a riot that broke out during the showing of a rock'n'roll film. Queen Elizabeth, concerned over the epidemic of riots that attended rock concerts, scheduled a private viewing of the film at her palace to study the problem. (Little did she suspect that within a few years she would be bestowing England's highest honors on a rock group—the Beatles.)

England's Bishop of Woolwich said rock'n'roll music had a "maddening effect on a rhythm-loving age group." Symphony conductor Sir Malcolm Sargent said, "It is nothing more than an exhibition of primitive tom-tom thumping."

Benny Goodman, whose hot clarinet had sparked riots among an earlier generation 20 years ago, said, "I guess it's okay, man. At least it has a beat."

One thing was obvious: this new music was emotional dynamite.

At first the kids weren't sure how to dance to this new music. Then Chubby Checker introduced the "Twist." It was followed by other rock dances, the "Frug," the "Watusi," the "Swim." The dance styles changed almost as fast as the chords of the music being played—but suddenly America had entered a new dancing age. Ballroom dancing and the jazz and swing steps had kept America out on the dance floor from the 1920's through the World War II years. But from the mid-forties on, we had lost interest in dancing. Well, there wasn't anything very exciting around to dance to. Then rock'n'roll came along and young people were on the dance floor again. But it was a whole new bag. Couples were not restricted to dancing cheek-to-cheek. Each partner was free to do his own thing. It gave the girls a new freedom. They did not have to submissively follow their male partner's lead.

So, despite the fuming of many adults, rock'n'roll was a solid hit. And the first victory the youth revolution achieved was to take over the pop music field. From the mid-1950's on, pop music was to be dominated by young entertainers. In a CBS Television special on rock music, Leonard Bernstein said that today's popular music scene is "unlike any scene I can think of in the history of all music. It's completely of, by, and for the kids, and by kids I mean anyone from eight years old to twenty-five. They write the songs, they sing them, own them, record them. They also buy the records, create the market, and they set the fashion in the music, in dress, in dance, in hair style, lingo, social attitudes."

High on popularity polls following the Elvis Presley revolution were Frankie Avalon with his hit, "Venus"; Fabian, "Turn Me Loose"; Little Anthony, "Tears on my Pillow"; Bobby Darin, "Mack the Knife"; Ricky Nelson, "Poor Little Fool"; and the Everly Brothers, "All I Have to Do Is Dream."

In the transition from pop to rock, a television music show that had been popular since the days of radio, "The Hit Parade," quietly expired. The disk jockey music show became the public forum for top chart tunes (which now rose and fell overnight. America's pop music tastes had reached a new high in fickleness). King of the deejays was Dick Clark, master of ceremonies for the afternoon TV show, "American Bandstand." Twenty million viewers watched the show every week. On the program, young fans danced as Clark played hit records of the week and introduced singers. Fabian, Bobby Darin and Connie Francis got their start on the Dick Clark show. Any recording played on the show was assured a marked climb on the popularity charts the following week.

A valid musical criticism of rock'n'roll is that it is repetitious, monotonous, and overly simplified. It has been compared to comic book culture. But hard rock is not intended to appeal to the esthetic sensibilities, nor to require the attention to musical finesse that jazz requires. It is basically anti-intellectual. It drowns the listener in a constant, pulsing beat, a beat so loudly amplified the shock waves can be felt. With the body moving to the steady command of the beat, a hypnotic effect is achieved. The senses blur, the world falls away. Everything is submerged in the primordal beat, perhaps the very heartbeat of the universe. Of course it is primitive. It appeals to something animal in all of us. It is not nearly as new a musical form as jazz. It goes back to the beginning of time. It is the cave man's hollow log drum plugged into a modern amplifier. It is ritualistic.

There have been many societies in which the ritualistic dance is seen, especially in connection with some religions. In some Indian religious ceremonies, participants dance themselves into a kind of mystic ecstacy. This type of hypnotic, rhythmic dancing is practiced in other cultures and other religions, too.

Taking these things into consideration, the phenomenon of rock'n'roll is not so unusual. It is a human experience that has been with us a long time—but has been brought up to date and intensified by modern electronics.

A glance over the top ten records for each year from 1950 through 1959 shows clearly the ascendancy of rock'n'roll and young singers in the pop music field:

1950

1. *Goodnight Irene*—The Weavers and Gordon Jenkins
2. *It Isn't Fair*—Sammy Kaye
3. *Third Man Theme*—Anton Karas

4. *Mule Train*—Frankie Laine
5. *Mona Lisa*—Nat "King" Cole
6. *Music! Music! Music!*—Teresa Brewer
7. *I Wanna Be Loved*—Andrew Sisters
8. *If I Knew You Were Comin' I'd've Baked a Cake*—Eileen Barton
9. *I Can Dream Can't I*—Andrew Sisters
10. *That Lucky Old Sun*—Frankie Laine

1951

1. *Tennessee Waltz*—Patti Page
2. *How High the Moon*—Les Paul and Mary Ford
3. *Too Young*—Nat "King" Cole
4. *Be My Love*—Mario Lanza
5. *Because of You*—Tony Bennett
6. *On Top of Old Smoky*—The Weavers and Gordon Jenkins
7. *If*—Perry Como
8. *Sin*—Eddy Howard
9. *Come On-a My House*—Rosemary Clooney
10. *Mockin' Bird Hill*—Patti Page

1952

1. *Cry*—Johnnie Ray
2. *Blue Tango*—Leroy Anderson
3. *Any Time*—Eddie Fisher
4. *Delicado*—Percy Faith
5. *Kiss of Fire*—Georgia Gibbs
6. *Wheel of Fortune*—Kay Starr
7. *Tell Me Why*—The Four Aces
8. *I'm Yours*—Don Cornell

9. *Here in My Heart*—Al Martino
10. *Auf Wierdersehen, Sweetheart*—Vera Lynn

1953

1. *Song from the Moulin Rouge*—Percy Faith
2. *Till I Waltz Again with You*—Teresa Brewer
3. *April in Portugal*—Lee Baxter
4. *Vaya Con Dios*—Les Paul and Mary Ford
5. *I'm Walking Behind You*—Eddie Fisher
6. *I Believe*—Frankie Laine
7. *You You You*—Ames Brothers
8. *Doggie in the Window*—Patti Page
9. *Why Don't You Believe Me*—Joni James
10. *Pretend*—Nat "King" Cole

1954

1. *Little Things Mean a Lot*—Kitty Kallen
2. *Hey There*—Rosemary Clooney
3. *Wanted*—Perry Como
4. *Young at Heart*—Frank Sinatra
5. *Sh-Boom*—The Crew Cuts
6. *Three Coins in the Fountain*—The Four Aces
7. *Little Shoemaker*—The Gaylords
8. *Oh! My Pa-Pa*—Eddie Fisher
9. *Secret Love*—Doris Day
10. *Happy Wanderer*—Frank Weir

1955

1. *Rock Around the Clock*—Bill Haley and the Comets
2. *Ballad of Davy Crockett*—Bill Hayes

3. *Cherry Pink and Apple Blossom White*—Perez Prado
4. *Melody of Love*—Billy Vaughn
5. *Yellow Rose of Texas*—Mitch Miller
6. *Ain't That a Shame*—Pat Boone
7. *Sincerely*—The McGuire Sisters
8. *Unchained Melody*—Les Baxter
9. *Crazy Otto Rag*—Crazy Otto
10. *Mister Sandman*—The Chordettes

1956

1. *Don't Be Cruel*—Elvis Presley
2. *Great Pretender*—The Platters
3. *My Prayer*—The Platters
4. *Wayward Wind*—Gogi Grant
5. *Whatever Will Be, Will Be*—Doris Day
6. *Heartbreak Hotel*—Elvis Presley
7. *Lisbon Antigua*—Nelson Riddle
8. *Canadian Sunset*—Hugo Winterhalter
9. *Moonglow* and *Theme from "Picnic"*—Morris Stoloff
10. *Honky Tonk*—Bill Doggett

1957

1. *Tammy*—Debbie Reynolds
2. *Love Letters in the Sand*—Pat Boone
3. *It's Not for Me to Say*—Johnny Mathis
4. *Young Love*—Tab Hunter
5. *Chances Are*—Johnny Mathis
6. *Little Darlin'*—The Diamonds
7. *Bye Bye Love*—The Everly Brothers
8. *All Shook Up*—Elvis Presley

9. *So Rare*—Jimmy Dorsey
10. *'Round and Round*—Perry Como

1958

1. *Volare*—Domenico Modugno
2. *It's All in the Game*—Tommy Edwards
3. *Patricia*—Perez Prado
4. *All I Have to Do Is Dream*—The Everly Brothers
5. *Bird Dog*—The Everly Brothers
6. *Little Star*—The Elegants
7. *Witch Doctor*—David Seville
8. *Twilight Time*—The Platters
9. *Tequila*—The Champs
10. *At the Hop*—Danny and The Juniors

1959

1. *Mack the Knife*—Bobby Darin
2. *Battle of New Orleans*—Johnny Horton
3. *Venus*—Frankie Avalon
4. *Lonely Boy*—Paul Anka
5. *There Goes My Baby*—The Drifters
6. *Personality*—Lloyd Price
7. *Three Bells*—The Browns
8. *Put Your Head on My Shoulder*—Paul Anka
9. *Sleep Walk*—Santo and Johnny
10. *Come Softly to Me*—The Fleetwoods

By the end of the 1950's, rock'n'roll was firmly entrenched in the growing youth culture. Adults were still grumbling about it and hoping that it would go away like a temporary fungus. But the up-coming decade—the 1960's—was to become the Rock Age.

The Beatles—*Capitol Records photo*

14   The Age of Rock

Whenever we review the events of the 1960 decade, we never fail to hear the throbbing of amplified guitars in the background. Hippies, long hair, civil rights marches, love-ins, flower children, surfing, black power, anti-war demonstrations, riots, LSD, Woodstock nation, communes, psychedelia, drug trips— these are all so inextricably involved with rock music that the decade virtually names itself: The Age of Rock.

When the first shock waves of the Elvis Presley rock music subsided in the early 1960's, American youth cast about for a new symbol on which to peg its music tastes. It came from Liverpool, England, in the person of four youngsters with sheep-dog hair styles who called themselves The Beatles. John Lennon, Paul McCartney, George Harrison and Ringo Starr. Like Elvis Presley, they dug the Negro blues singers, Muddy Waters, Bo Diddley and Chuck Berry. But they added a lighter note of whimsey which became known as the Mersey sound (Liverpool, overlooking the Mersey River, is the pop music capital of England).

The early songs of the Beatles had a positive, cheerful quality, departing from the heavier mood of the blues. Their early hit recordings were "Love Me

195

Do," and "She Loves You," and the very big, "I Want to Hold Your Hand." This was in 1963. In 1964, they appeared on the Ed Sullivan show, drew the largest audience in television history, and sent a whole new generation of adolescent girls into screaming, fainting ecstacy. They also set the trends in hair, clothes, and life styles for teenagers all over the world. The barbershop suddenly became a place to be avoided by youngsters in Tokyo, Berlin, Los Angeles, Rome, and most other cities and hamlets in the world. In the year 1964 alone, the Beatles earned some fourteen million dollars, and Queen Elizabeth decorated them with the Order of the British Empire for their success in boosting British exports.

John Lennon, Paul McCartney and George Harrison first got together in 1956 when they were teenagers. They were born in the seaport town of Liverpool of lower or middle class backgrounds. Probably this accounts for their put-down of the upper classes. They dressed and wore their hair in a way to make fun, by overstatement, of the appearances of educated Eton boys. At a Royal Command Performance in London, John Lennon told the audience, "People in the cheap seats can clap. The rest of you—rattle your jewelry."

They started out as musical illiterates, none of them being able to read or write music. Since then they have studied music, but their method of composing remains spontaneous.

In 1962, drummer Richard Starkey, known to the world as Ringo Starr, joined the group and they produced their first album, *Meet the Beatles* in 1964. A series of albums followed, culminating in their thirteenth, *Sergeant Pepper's Lonely Hearts Club Band,* which contains some advanced dissonant sounds and electronic techniques. (In today's music, the studio electronic engineer has become as important a member of the performing team as the violin or brass section. Probably more so.)

During the years the group recorded together as the Beatles, they either knowingly, or by accident, used such musical devices as Medieval modes, pentatonic scales, baroque styles, classical string quartet and the Indian sitar. Some music critics pontificate in great detail on the importance and intricacies of Beatle compositions, comparing them to the great classical composers. Time will tell if this is true. It may turn out they were simply a little group of popular song writers and performers who were having a good time.

Parents felt a bit less apprehensive about the Beatles than they had about Elvis. True, the Beatles were a fast-talking, wacky group who put everybody down, but they did it in such a cheerful, disarming manner that nobody got mad at them. Besides, despite the long hair, they looked so neat and *clean.*

Meanwhile, another group in England was attracting attention. Led by Mick Jagger, they called themselves the Rolling Stones. A scruffy, scroungy looking crew, they were as dirty as the Beatles were clean. Where the Beatles maintained a wholesome air about their performing, the Rolling Stones played up the dark, primitive qualities of rock. They came on like something out of the zoo and looked as if they never took a bath. They played what has been termed "heavy rock."

Actually, they played up this animal appeal to

their advantage. Their manager, 20-year-old pop music promoter Andrew Loog Oldham, emphasized their unsavory reputation on the theory that the more the adults disapproved of the Stones, the more the kids, wrapped up in the youth rebellion against the older generation, would dig them. Thus the Rolling Stones with their heavy rock and emphasis on sex became the leading symbols for the "anti-establishment" crowd. And Mick Jagger, leader of the group, joined Bob Dylan, James Dean and Elvis Presley as a folk hero of the young.

Despite competition from a horde of rock groups and "superstars," the Beatles and the Rolling Stones dominated the rock-pop music scene for most of the 1960's. Along with them, at the top of the heap, with $85-million in records sales has been the group, Creedence Clearwater Revival.

Mick Jagger came from a comfortable, middle-class home. His father was a physical-education instructor. In 1962, when he was 18, Mick Jagger was attending the London School of Economics, but spent all his free time listening to blues records from black America. Chuck Berry, Bo Diddley, Fats Domino and Muddy Waters were his heroes. Then Mick joined with Keith Richard, Charlie Watts and Bill Wyman, formed a band and began hustling for engagements. Soon, like the Beatles, they were playing for screaming, fainting mobs. Jagger and Keith Richard began writing their own songs, and by 1964, they were crowding the Beatles for top spot in the rock world. But the Stones, unlike the Beatles, kept their style closer to a direct imitation of the heavy, black rhythm'n'blues roots. The spotlight was always on Jagger with his prancing, dynamic style and his obvious and often vulgar sexual gestures.

Everything about the Rolling Stones, their private lives as well as their performances, was a direct sneer at the civilized, adult world. To watch them was to watch 4,000 years of civilization go down the drain. But the youth movement, seething with a deep, dark malaise, identified with them. In the words of a *Newsweek* report, "the Stones precipitated a turned-on frenzy and unleashed a submerged rebelliousness in both boys and girls as no other group did."

With success came problems for the Stones in their own lives. In 1967, Mick, Keith Richard and Brian Jones were arrested on drug charges. Mick was sentenced to three months in prison and Keith Richard to one year, but a higher court set aside Richard's conviction and reduced Mick's to a probationary sentence. Brian Jones did not have to serve any time in prison; they found him dead in his swimming pool one morning.

A good example of the Stones in action can be heard on the album, *Flowers,* London PS 509.

Meanwhile, in the U.S., rock was developing in several directions. Early in the 1960's, from California, came the Surfing Sound, made popular by the Beach Boys. Their music had a light, staccato quality and dealt with high school dating, cars, drag racing and surfing. An example of their style can be heard on the album *Surfin' Safari,* Capitol DT 1808.

The Motown Sound (short for "motor town"— Detroit) smacks a lot more of rhythm'n'blues. It has much heavy rhythm, passionate, emotional shouting and shrieking, wild saxophones. Some call it "schlock rock." The Supremes, James Brown, Martha and the Vandellas are exponents of this style. A good album to listen to is *The Motown Sound,* Volume 6, Motown S 655.

Hard rock has dominated the rock field during most of the 1960's. It is straight-forward, no nonsense, hard-driving and loud, loud, loud. Both the playing and singing have a primitive, rough-edged quality which often substitutes for musical talent.

Psychedelic rock, sometimes called West Coast, the Nitty-Gritty and the San Francisco sound emerged from the drug-hallucination, acid-trip scene. It blossomed among San Francisco's hippie culture and was given expression on week-ends in such immense ballrooms as Bill Graham's Fillmore Auditorium, the Avalon Ballroom, and college auditoriums like the Pauley Ballroom at Berkeley. Total sound from amplifiers at peak volume makes the building quiver like salvos from giant field cannon. At the same time, strobe lights, pulsing to the beat, assault the eyes. Psychedelic projections of protoplasmic blobs and spidery tendrils slither over the walls. It's freaked-out. It's turned-on. It rakes at the nerves and drenches the senses. The idea is to produce a simulated LSD trip by this concerted attack on the senses.

Psychedelic bands sprang up like fungi in a damp cellar. They were a great unkempt, unwashed tribe who generally had more enthusiasm than talent. Nightclubs around the country hopped on the fad, giving light shows along with loud, hard rock, attracting hoards of young people in hippie regalia and bare feet (a mode of attire that started out as a rebellion against conformity and wound up the most stringent kind of uniform. Anyone daring to show up with a hair cut, suit and tie would have been looked upon as a way-out kind of freak).

Out of the hundreds of amateur groups, a few gained national recognition and hit top record charts —the Jefferson Airplane, the Grateful Dead, the Quicksilver Messenger Service, Big Brother and the Holding Company, the Sopwith "Camel," the 13th Floor Elevator, Country Joe and the Fish, and the Loading Zone.

The San Francisco sound feeds on various sources of current pop music—the Beatles, folk, country, the blues. And, in the mid-sixties, the Indian Raga was incorporated into the rock sounds. How such an unlikely musical form as the raga crept into the pop scene came about this way: in 1965, George Harrison of the Beatles heard some records by Ravi Shankar, one of India's foremost virtuosos of the sitar. Harrison made a trip to India and studied with Shankar for six weeks. That same year, the Beatles produced their recording, *Norwegian Wood,* which contained some hints of the sitar. Later, their *Strawberry Fields Forever* and *Penny Lane* made much more of the sitar sound. A group called the Byrds recorded *Eight Miles High* which they identified as "raga rock" and another group, the Doors, produced *The End* which has a sitar solo lasting 11 minutes and 35 seconds.

Suddenly, the sitar was very much "in." For a while Ravi Shankar, who toured America giving concerts with his raga troupe, became a new pied piper of the rock set.

The sitar is a formidable looking instrument with 19 strings and an impressive number of knobs for tuning. Indian music, with its vast number of scales as well as different divisions of the octave, sounds utterly foreign to most of us, and the sitar produces a sound something like a bucket of steel needles being spilled on a tin roof while a tight rubber band twangs. How such an unlikely instrument and its music became a rock institution is one of those inexplicable mysteries of American popular music fads. Probably the explanation lies in the fact that pop music fans are constantly seeking a new "sound" and in the sitar they found it—at least until the next thing comes along.

With drugs so much a part of the youth scene, especially the hallucinogens such as marijuana, LSD and peyote, it was almost inevitable the subject would creep into pop music lyrics. As a result, there was quite a flap during the 1960's over radio stations and record manufacturers cleaning up these songs. The problem was in deciphering the lyrics. The youngsters who sang and listened to the songs had developed a language all their own, and often they alone understood the double entendre of the words.

For example, "Puff the Magic Dragon," innocuous enough on the surface, could mean smoking pot. When Bob Dylan sings "Ev'rybody Must Get Stoned," the parents might conjure up a mental picture of throwing rocks, while "getting stoned" to the hip generation is to be high on drugs or alcohol. And the title of the song, "Rainy Day Woman" is a hip code for marijuana cigarette. The Jefferson Airplane number, "Running Around the World," can be interpreted to mean the experience of love-making while under the influence of LSD.

Rock'n'roll has always had its raunchy overtones, and the lyrics often have sexual meanings. Many radio stations launched a campaign against such songs as the Rolling Stones' "Let's Spend the Night Together," the Detroit Wheels' "Sock it to Me, Baby," or Lou Christie's "Rhapsody in the Rain."

A group called the Fugs are so explicit in their titles and words that even squares have no difficulty in getting the meaning. They lay it on the line. But in most cases, the problem radio stations and record companies have is that first of all, the meaning of the words is obscured by teenage jargon, and secondly, the way the singers scream their vocals, nobody but teenagers seem to know what they are saying. So, the rock bands continue to put out records which may deal with drugs, sex, and anarchism, if you can translate their meaning. This has become known as underground rock.

Attacks on The Establishment are expressed in many of the rock and folk-rock lyrics. Some spokesmen for the rock generation say the very music itself with its hyped-up volume, primitive beat and emotion is a more explicit cry against The Establishment than any words accompanying the tunes.

Along in the late 1960's there appeared a renewed interest in the blues roots of rock. Some called it a "blues revival." Bill Graham, owner-promoter of the two Carnegie Halls of rock, the Fillmore East and Fillmore West, presented many of the old-time country blues singers. The Electric Circus in New York put on a series of blues concerts featuring such living creators of the blues as Bukka White, Muddy Waters, Mama Thorton, Son House, Junior Wells, and John Lee Hooker.

A strong blues influence began to be heard in rock groups such as the Paul Butterfield Blues Band, the Blues Project, the Steve Miller Blues Band, the Charley Musselwhite Blues Band, Ten Years After, Canned Heat, Steppenwolf, Creedence Clearwater Revival and Blood Sweat and Tears.

The two individual performers who burst upon the rock scene in this era of blues revival and became for a brief period the superstars of rock music were a young white girl from Port Arthur, Texas, Janis Joplin, and a young black hippie from Seattle, Jimi Hendrix.

Back in her home in Port Arthur, Janis Joplin was bored by the pop music of the 1950's until she heard blues singer Leadbelly. Then she collected Bessie Smith records and became totally committed to the Negro blues music. She left home and struck out for the hippie haven of San Francisco's North Beach, with no real intention of becoming a singer; she only wanted to be one of the street people. But she sang with Big Brother and the Holding Company, and then she appeared at the 1967 Monterey International Pop Festival and the whole rock music world went wild over her. To say she sang with intense passion and emotion would be a pallid understatement. Her singing has been described as "a desperate mating call." Certainly, she wrung every bit of sex out of each song —a performance that left both her and the audience limp.

Jimi Hendrix sang with his own brand of hyped-up intensity. Unfortunately, both these performers fell victims to the mad, driving pace of their music and their way-out drug-oriented life styles. By the end of the decade they had both died within days of each other of drug overdoses.

A curious twist to the career of Jimi Hendrix is that he was posthumously elected to the *Down Beat* Jazz Hall of Fame by its readers. *Down Beat* is a jazz-committed publication and its followers do not generally consider rock music or rock musicians a part of the jazz scene. Nevertheless, there was apparently enough of the innovator and improvisor in Hendrix to qualify him as a jazz musician in the minds of *Down Beat* readers. You may decide for yourself by listening to Hendrix on Reprise-Ampex tapes, "Are You Experienced," "Bold as Love," "Electric Lady-land," and "Live at Monterey Album." Also, he can be heard on the Cotillion-Ampex tape, "Woodstock."

Another idol of rock between the years of 1968 and 1971 was Jim Morrison of The Doors. Rock music, which started with the writhings of "Elvis the Pelvis," has always had raunchy overtones. Jim Morrison's unsavory reputation—he was once arrested in Miami Beach for his allegedly lewd performance while singing with the band—rated him right at the top of the purveyors of "dirty style." He reportedly once began a rock concert by telling the audience of his latest sexual exploits. His concerts have been compared to the Greek orgiastic rites to the pagan god of lust and wine, Dionysus. Nevertheless, the Doors are highly regarded in the rock music world and their album *The Doors*, Elektra, EKS 74007, was described by the rock magazine, *Crawdaddy*, as ". . . the most powerfully controlled release of accumulated instrumental kineticism on record."

Jim Morrison, the daddy of Sexbomb Rock, joined Janis Joplin and Jimi Hendrix in their headlong rush to self-destruction. He was twenty-seven when he died in Paris, in July, 1971. Cause of death was given as "natural causes."

It may not be altogether fair to blame the hippie-drug-sex scene of rock music for taking the lives of so many of its top young performers. The entertainment field has always carried the seeds of self-destruction. In the country-western field, Hank Williams was not much older than Jim Morrison when he died. Back in the hot jazz era, Bix Beiderbecke died at the ripe young age of twenty-eight, his body demolished by dissipation and prohibition booze. However, the rock music field does make excruciating demands on its "stars." The surge to stardom can come overnight. Then the performer becomes both the idol and the victim of his screaming, adulating fans. With no compromise, they savagely demand something new, something more. In clawing his fingers bloody at those top charts, he stretches his talent and his health to the breaking point. Being young, he has not yet learned how to do anything in moderation or to pace himself. There is only one way he knows to live—as intensely as he plays and sings his souped-up, screaming music. Sometimes it is more than the human body and nervous system were designed to cope with.

In this same vein, hard rock produced some rather troublesome physical problems for both performers and audience. Ear specialists discovered that audiences constantly exposed to powerful rock amplifiers producing sounds above 90 decibels were suffering permanent hearing loss. One of the researchers in this field is Dr. George T. Singleton, head of the division of otolaryngology, University of Florida. He found the music ranged from 120 decibels at the bandstand to 106 decibels at the center of the dance floor. He tested his daughter and nine other teenagers before and after a rock concert and found a measurable hearing loss in all. After only a few exposures to the high noise level, the loss is generally recovered, but many experts believe repeated listening leads to permanent hearing damage.

Singers of rock'n'roll have their own problems. The style of screaming the lyrics loudly, often in abnormally high pitches in a falsetto voice, plus the emotional frenzy that goes along with the singing, puts a damaging strain on the vocal chords. Dr. Eugene M. Batza of the Cleveland Clinic's otolaryngology department told the *Chicago Daily News* in an interview, "The risk of permanent degenerative changes is present. The enormous popularity of these musicians makes exhausting demands on them. Some groups perform almost every evening and for some there are recording sessions, frequent rehearsals and considerable arduous travel from engagement to engagement.

"They rely on their youthful resiliency to carry them through, but they would do well to remember that singing is a physical activity. Abuse of the pitching arm, particularly after fatigue noticeably has set in, can be catastrophic to the serious athlete."

He explained that few rock'n'roll singers are

professionally trained and consequently have not a systematic development of the vocal chords as opera singers do. Batza examined a group of five prominent rock musicians who had been singing professionally for five years. All five showed traumatic laryngitis, bilateral vocal cord nodules and a horny growth on the cords.

The problems accompanying 120 decibel music may resolve themselves. Judging by the top popularity polls at the end of the 1960's, hard rock was "out" and new soft sounds are "in." The top five selections nominated for the 1970 Record of the Year award went to softer, melodic renditions: "Bridge Over Troubled Water" by Simon and Garfunkel; "Close to You," by the Carpenters; "Everything is Beautiful," by Ray Stevens; "Fire and Rain," by James Taylor, and "Let it Be," by the Beatles.

The chief criticism of the rock-pop of the 1960's must be directed at the low quality of musicianship of the performers and the gimmicky aspect of the whole music scene. However, let me hasten to add that other types of pop music have their short-comings too. The swing era had its great bands such as Woody Herman and Count Basie, but it also had the commercial foolishness of Kay Kyser's College of Musical Knowledge, and Shep Field's Rippling Rhythm, not to mention idiotic songs like "Marizy Doats." Some country music might be of honest folk value, but along side it are the drug store cowboy dress styles and all the razz-ma-tazz of pastel colored Cadillacs with steerhorns mounted on the hoods. So every generation and every style has its own particular kind of silliness. That is a part of popular music.

It does not aim to please music critics, but to satisfy the general public. And rock music particularly appeals to an immature audience from eight years of age to the early twenties.

However, since the rock styles have become so widespread throughout our culture and since it is the most important music of an entire generation, it must answer to critical observations. One of its main shortcomings has been its dependence upon gimmicks. Off-beat costumes and silly names, strobe lights, the movements of the performers on the stage, their attitude—these became as important to the success of a rock group as the music it played. More dependence was placed on the electronic equipment a musician could muster than on his training or skill as a performer. "If you can't play good, play loud," was the theory of most rock'n'rollers. I recently attended a "battle of the bands" in which twenty amateur rock bands competed for a cash prize. Afterwards, I heard one of the losers say that he must buy some larger speakers and stronger amplifiers because he felt sure that would give him a better chance next time. He said nothing about improving himself as a musician. In his honest opinion, his worth as a musician hinged on the number of watts his amplifier could produce. The joke that to produce a successful rock musician, one needs $2,000 worth of equipment combined with three cents worth of talent, has some basis in fact.

Concern for the state of musicianship of young people was voiced in an article in the May, 1971, issue of the *Instrumentalist* magazine by Floyd Werle. Sergeant Werle is Chief Arranger for the U.S. Air Force Band, Symphony Orchestra and Singing Sergeants.

He has written numerous band transcriptions and
has contributed original scores for 12 motion pictures. In his article, he makes the following observations:

"The very prevalence of rock in our society has
frightening implications for the band and those band
directors who regard themselves as educators. Why
have we failed to learn lessons which should have
been learned back in the Swing Era, when a goodly
percentage of us were kids, ourselves?

"More than one generation of us, myself included, struggled dutifully with Bach and Beethoven
at the piano and with equivalent wind-instrument
fodder, but failed to gain any insight or understanding of this music until after exposure to the mechanics of the pop culture of our day. 'Boogie-woogie' and
like arts having been summarily rejected by the
'music educators' in the hallowed high school halls,
our real teachers became the leaders and sidemen of
the various dance orchestras we worked with. Thirty
years too late, the 'stage band' is doing what should
have been done then. . . .

"One factor, however, was working for us then
which is not working for anybody now. Though
vehemently denied by the 'music educators' of that
day, Benny Goodman, Tommy Dorsey, Harry James
and the other idols were genuine virtuosi on their
instruments and as a result we did learn to play. Today we contend with a new generation of 'music educators' (maybe even the same generation) whom we
need to ask, in all seriousness, why the flourishing
rock bands have to learn their material by rote and
experimentation one rigorous chord at a time, why

it can take eight solid hours to get just one three-minute tape in the can, and why the cost of producing a single hit LP can easily exceed one hundred thousand dollars. We need to ask them why acid-heads and dope addicts are emulated over the genuinely talented players brought in for overdubbing sessions to make these idols look good. We need to ask an embarrassing percentage of them if what they are actually dispensing in our schools can be defined as either music or education. Never has a country had such an appetite for music as ours and been so poorly equipped to play the music it genuinely wants to play and hear. . . ."

But with all that is said about the shortcomings of rock, and much of this valid criticism, the fact remains that rock music has a vitality, power and excitement that other pop music forms lack. And it has been the most important form of expression for an entire generation. This alone makes it a very powerful force in our culture. It has outlasted many other music trends and will very likely continue to be around in one form or another for quite some time to come. The direction rock is taking these days appears to be toward better musical values. If this trend continues we may well be headed for a time when pop music is better than ever.

A still from "Woodstock"—*photo,
courtesy Warner Brothers, Inc., and
George Nichols*

15 Rise and Fall of the Rock Festivals

Rock music knew its golden hour on a rented 600-acre dairy farm near the town of Woodstock, New York, in the summer of 1969. There, 400,000 young people gathered for the three day Woodstock Festival which was to make history as the super love-in of all time. The weather was miserable. Rainstorms turned the countryside into a giant mud quagmire. Food was lacking, shelter and sanitation were at a minimum, or non-existent. But despite the inconvenience and discomfort, there was no trouble, no fights, nothing to mar that glorious epic of fun and laughter and love and music.

The music was the greatest as far as the crowd was concerned. The line-up of bands and superstars sounded like a rock music hall of fame: Joan Baez, Butterfield Blues Band, Canned Heat, Joe Cocker, Country Joe and the Fish, Crosby, Stills, Nash and Young, Arlo Guthrie, Jimi Hendrix, Jefferson Airplane, Country Joe McDonald, Santana, John B. Sebastian, Sha-na-na, Sly and the Family Stone, Ten Years After, the Who, Melanie, and Moutain. It can all be heard on the 3-record Cotillion album set, SD 3–500, titled *Woodstock,* and on Cotillion SD 2–400, *Woodstock Two.*

The crowd was young—15 to 25 for the most part. They sang, danced, drank beer, smoked pot, went swimming. If somebody wanted to take all his clothes off, it was groovy. Weren't they all one big, happy family?

No one who was there will ever forget it. Nothing that has happened in recent times can quite compare with it. This is what the world should be like. This was what all the great religious leaders and prophets had in mind: a world filled with love and concern for one another. A banishment of prejudice, hatred, violence.

Yes, it was fine. There were a few freaked-out kids who were on bum LSD trips. Nothing is ever *completely* perfect. But enough of it was so good, the young generation could call themselves the Woodstock Nation. They had a right to have a supreme feeling about the whole scene. And rock'n'roll, their music, had been the heartbeat of the whole event.

It was not the only successful rock festival. Two years before, the historic 1967 International Pop Festival in Monterey, California, had among other things, introduced Janis Joplin to the rock world. In the same summer as Woodstock, 1969, some 200,000 young people gathered on the Isle of Wight off the coast of England to hear Bob Dylan.

But Woodstock had been the best. It was hailed as the start of the millenium.

Sadly, though, after Woodstock, it all started going sour. Just four months after Woodstock, the Rolling Stones climaxed their U.S. tour with a free rock concert in Altamont, California. It turned into a nightmare. The crowd was in a troublesome mood, trying in their zeal to push closer and closer. A band of Hell's Angels, hired for $500 worth of beer to maintain order, ran amuck, beating the crowd back with weighted pool cues. When the band played, it turned the crowd on to greater frenzy. Mick Jagger stopped the music repeatedly, begging the crowd to calm down, threatening to leave. But he played again and the ugly scene like the tail-end of an LSD nightmare ground to a bloody finish as the Hell's Angel bunch knifed and stomped to death a black man who was brandishing a gun.

The glory that had been Woodstock was short-lived. The innocence of the whole movement died at Altamont. Again the powerful, volatile energy generated by rock had been demonstrated. When a crowd gathers, rock is more than music. It is a force. It can be a force for good as at Woodstock, or, if it gets out of hand, pure destruction as at Altamont. Tensions generated by rock can explode.

Disillusionment with the rock scene set in. Success of the outdoor festivals turned sour. As often as not, the crowd broke through gates and stampeded in without paying. Or tore up the place if the rock bands did not appear as promised.

In an Associated Press interview, Richard Bryan, a sponsor of the Atlanta International Pop Festival in Byron, Georgia, said, "Eventually, people are going through the gate free. It's not a point of whether, but of when; the question is whether you'll break even before they do."

The Randall Island Festival in New York City was so besieged by radicals that the doors were thrown open to the public. Promoter of the festival,

Don Friedman, said, "The love-peace thing of Woodstock has gone out. It's been replaced by anarchy—
complete, total anarchy."

In 1970, Jon Northland, assistant editor of the
leading rock weekly magazine *Rolling Stone* said that
out of 48 major festivals scheduled, only 18 actually
came off.

Local and state governments were often responsible for halting the promotion of rock festivals. In
some states, such as in Texas, state governments
were busy passing legislation to curtail outdoor concerts.

The decline of rock festivals was only one of
many indications that the era of hard rock was fading out at the end of the 1960's and we may be in
for some new trends in music. Rock music has depended on its heroes and symbols for much of its
success. Janis Joplin, Jimi Hendrix, Jim Morrison
are dead. Bob Dylan, a comfortable millionaire, is no
longer the fiery protest writer he was in the early
1960's. And the Beatles' partnership ended in Room
16 of the London Law Courts.

The two great emporia of rock, Fillmore East
in New York and Fillmore West in San Francisco,
closed in the early summer of 1971. It would be hard
to think of anything more significant. Columnist William Buckley compared it to the Catholic Church
closing down Lourdes.

The rock impresario-owner of the two Fillmores,
Bill Graham, blamed the closing on the high pay demanded by performing groups. Bands like Sly and
the Jefferson Airplane get fees as high as $50,000 for
a single night's performance. In an Associated Press

interview written by Joel Dreyfuss, Bill Graham said the matter of income has become more important to the musicians than music. "Rock is joining America. It's becoming a General Motors, a Pacific Gas and Electric or any other big corporation you can name. When we started in 1965, I associated with and employed musicians. Now more often than not, it's with officers and stockholders in large corporations, only they happen to have long hair and play guitars."

That is an ironic turn of events for a kind of music that began as the pulse of the anti-establishment movement.

Another new direction is that the songs in which a few years ago the young were demanding instant change and instant power have become resigned to the fact that the world doesn't change so easily. Back in 1969, Jimi Hendrix in a *Newsweek* interview said, "Lots of young people now feel that they're not getting a fair deal. So they revert to something loud and harsh, almost verging on violence; if they don't go to a (rock) concert, they might be going to a riot." And in a rock concert in Chicago in 1968, Jim Morrison yelled, "We want the world, now, now, now!"

Inasmuch as the world was not forthcoming "now,now,now" the Doors were, by the time of Morrison's death, singing a different tune on their hit record "Riders on the Storm." They compared themselves to a dog without a bone as they were cast onto the earth. Even the Rolling Stones are now singing, "You Can't Always Get What You Want."

Perhaps sobered by the drug-deaths of so many rock stars, many of the groups appear to be turning away from drug-oriented lyrics. In an Associated

Press interview by Gene Handsaker, Mike Curb, president of MGM Records says, "There's a real trend against drug music. It's very encouraging. In times past we've seen countless groups walk in here just bombed out of their minds. Some groups didn't like drugs, but felt they had to be on them to be more 'in.'" He announced that MGM would no longer release any records "advocating the use of drugs." He further stated the record company would refuse to give any hard-drug addicts recording contracts no matter how many records their names might sell.

The most significant event to befall the rock music world as the 1960's drew to a close was the Beatles' separation. It was their group that had continuously dazzled the pop world. They were the seminal force of the rock music of the 1960's. Before the decade ended, they had split up musically and by the early 1970's were in the process of dissolving their final business ties.

Friction in the group had been going on for several years. McCartney who liked pop styles squabbled with John Lennon who went in for underground with its disguised meanings. "Lucy in the Sky with Diamonds," for example, can be translated to mean a song about an LSD trip. Feuding also went on between Paul McCartney and George Harrison. Harrison claimed that McCartney insisted on telling him how to play guitar. Once, during the filming of *Let It Be* in 1969, the argument became so heated, Harrison threatened to split. That fuss was patched up, but the rifts grew wider.

By 1971, the Beatles who had once functioned so well as a unit, giving the world tunes like "Yesterday" and "Michelle," were each putting out their own records and getting involved in a rating battle among themselves. George Harrison, youngest of the group, held top spot on the charts for seven weeks with his pop hymn, "My Sweet Lord." By March of 1971, world sales of the record were over three million. But Harrison lost his top chart position to Paul McCartney who, with his American wife, Linda Eastman, wrote "Another Day." At the same time, John Lennon and the Plastic Ono Band were in the charts and climbing with "Power to the People."

In the early years, Harrison had been overshadowed by Lennon and McCartney who had been the song-writing team of the Beatles. But now on his own, Harrison has developed a new style and has become an international star. His triple record album, *All Things Must Pass*, has been a highly successful seller throughout the world. It has a religious tone. Harrison came from a Roman Catholic family. He rejected religion in his teens, but recently found a renewed interest in everything from Oriental mysticism to Christianity. It shows up in his songs.

The fourth Beatle, Ringo Starr, has been doing his own thing, too, making films and a country-western album in Nashville, Tennessee.

The Beatles probably got along best when they were a young group, just starting out, making it up the hard route of one-night stands, struggling to gain recognition. When they had a quarrel, they took a vote. A majority of three made the decision. Then, too, they had manager Brian Epstein who seemed to know best how to smooth over quarrels and patch up hurt egos. He was the father image to the group. But he died from an overdose of sleeping pills in August, 1967, and from then on, the Beatles drifted apart. They hired Allen Klein as their business manager in May, 1969. Klein, an American, was credited by Lennon, Harrison and Starr for saving the group from bankruptcy. McCartney, however, made it clear that he never did trust Klein.

The Beatles' partnership is a company called the Apple Corps. Lennon is quoted as saying, in a Newspaper Enterprise Association article by Tom Cullen, that the Apple Corps had become corrupt with "spongers and hustlers." He observed that the staff "came and went as they pleased." Two of the Apple's automobiles had completely disappeared, said Lennon, and they discovered they owned a house "which no one can remember buying."

Allan Klein straightened all that out, but he was not able to bring harmony back to the Beatles themselves. McCartney named the other three as defendants in a lawsuit which sought to dissolve the partnership. Lennon, Starr and Harrison were not in a big hurry to call it quits, for a very practical reason. As long as their earnings go into the corporation, they enjoy a considerable tax protection. Once this is dissolved, each Beatle may be liable for a surtax bite of 88.75 per cent of their income.

But the end of the Beatles appears inevitable. The last flimsy ties, the business structure of their corporation, is being dissolved by court action. It is sad; it marks the end of an era in pop music.

16   Where Does It Go From Here?

It is difficult to predict the future development of popular music with certainty, but it is possible to make some educated guesses.

I believe it is safe to say that in spite of some of the unfortunate things that happened to rock at the end of the 1960's, it will be around for some time to come. It may not be as loud, and the public may grow weary of some of the gimmicks which are by now rather tired clichés. But the basic idea of the beat and rhythm will no doubt survive and influence pop music styles for quite some time. The exuberance and drive of rock is too good to discard.

Some of the adolescent ego-tripping and teenage conformity may leave the rock scene. The drop-outs of the 1960's—kids from middle-class homes—will be approaching thirty, and somehow sleeping in doorways and blowing one's mind on turned-on sound grows less attractive as middle-age approaches. The anti-establishment kids are beginning to have families and settle down to the kind of work they like. The huge "baby boom" of post World War II years is maturing into young family units. The top-heavy population ratio of young people is shifting. Often, as teenagers reach late twenties, they out-grow the

221

teeny-bopper stage of hard and heavy rock. Their cultural tastes broaden to include music they once considered square.

How about jazz? Some writers predict a renaissance of jazz. Others predict a marriage of jazz and rock. To date, experiments along that line have not been very successful. Blood Sweat and Tears has done the best job of bringing the "big band" sound to rock, and it has reintroduced instruments other than guitars to the pop music field. In all likelihood, the rock groups will make increasing use of wind instruments, perhaps once again whole brass and reed sections.

An interesting development has been the rock musical and opera. *Hair* and *Jesus Christ, Superstar* have enjoyed great success. The strong emotions that can be expressed through rock music adapt well to dramatic opera. A whole new approach to a popular form of opera may grow out of the rock movement. It could bring a new vitality to the opera form and make it more interesting to the general public. At least the possibility is there.

One does not take a great risk in predicting that country-western will continue to grow in popularity. As the Nashville Sound becomes increasingly smooth, it will appeal to a wider audience.

There appears to be a growing trend toward an amalgamation of rock, country-western and soul. Perhaps there is more of a likelihood that the "new music" of the 1970's will grow out of that combination than a combination of rock and jazz.

So much depends upon the condition in which the world finds itself and the events we experience.

These are the elements that shape popular music. In the 1960's we went to the extremes in sexual permissiveness, drugs, youth rebellion and violence. The pendulum may swing the other way. Things often go in cycles. We may enter an era of conservatism, restraint, sentimentality. Good manners may return. If that is the case, pop music may go through a more subtle, reflective period.

An encouraging sign appears to be a growing emphasis on better musicianship. We may be returning to a time when one has to have more than three weeks of lessons on a guitar to become a pop music star.

Another matter to consider is the ratio of young people to those over thirty. In the 1960's, the world belonged to the young if for no other reason than that they had everyone else outnumbered. But as increasing emphasis is placed on family planning, and as medical science improves not only the span but the quality of the mature years, we may be coming up with a time when the young will be in a decided minority. This conjures up some interesting speculations. Age sits quite well on the shoulders of jazz musicians. Most of the members of Duke Ellington's band are in their fifties or sixties, yet this does not detract from their stage presence or performance. Indeed, many jazz musicians mellow and improve their styles as they become senior citizens. At Preservation Hall in New Orleans, most of the performers are in their seventies. They may have to sit down when they play, but they swing with all the fire of youth, and the audience loves them. But will the same be true of the rock performers? Will the kids of the

1960's, on their golden anniversary somewhere in the misty future, groove to a recording of the Rolling Stones screaming "Gimmie Shelter?" Will grey haired senior citizens in some retirement home in the year 2020, be doing the frug to recordings of Jefferson Airplane, replayed at 120 decibels? Somehow a vision of a grey-haired, paunchy Elvis swinging his hips and singing "You Ain't Nothin' But A Hound Dog" boggles the imagination.

All the branches of pop music that people listen to today—the mellow songs of Frank Sinatra, the big-band sounds left over from the 1930's, the show tunes, sound tracks from movies, rock, folk, blues and country-western, and the great jazz bands—give us all a broad musical fare to choose from. No matter what our tastes in music may be, somewhere we can find music we like. And that is really the only test popular music need answer to. That's what will decide the directions popular music will take in the future. Pop music couldn't care less what critics think about it, so long as it is "easy to understand, plain, adapted to the means of the generality of the people, having general currency, and beloved or approved by the people."